Everyone in the church needs to not only read this book, but to study and intentionally apply its principles. David Anderson does an excellent job exposing us to the disabled who most often are hidden from view. This practical, biblically-grounded text will tear down barriers between people with and without disabilities, and help us (the church) discover how we must minster *to* and *with* persons and families dealing with disabilities.

Donald Mortenson, D. Min., Pastor of Congregational Care, Marriage & Family Ministries, Whittier Area Community Church. Adjunct Professor Bethel Theological Seminary (formally Associate Professor of Pastoral Care)

Having been in the world of disabilities my entire life—as son, brother, nephew, friend, caregiver, and more—I can vouch for *Reaching Out and Bringing In* as a book equally valuable to the disabled community and to those who minister within that community. David has described here what is instinctive for me and many others.

This book captures the truth about all people in the eyes of God their Creator and refutes humanly manufactured prejudice regarding people with external differences and disabilities that creates social separation and enslaves both those with disabilities and the able-bodied. I have traveled with David internationally and his keen Bible knowledge and understanding of humanity as the Creator sees us has been used by Christ to change many lives.

Reaching Out and Bringing In has excited me as no other disability ministry book has; it is an honor to call David a friend as well as co-worker in the harvest fields of Christ. I strongly recommend *Reaching Out and Bringing In* as a must-read for those who minister to and with persons with disabilities, and even as a Bible study for all Christians.

Dana Croxton, founder of *Enable Ministries*—Training the Body of Christ for In-home Care of the Ill, Injured and Disabled as Evangelism.

Reaching Out and Bringing In, by David Anderson, is a relatively short and very accessible book of "pastoral theology" related to disability. It is theology because it asks the big "why" questions about disability, and provides balanced answers to many of them. It is pastoral in that it doesn't present the theology in just an academic sense. Rather, it speaks to many of the common questions about disability, in a way that fosters practical ministry. It provides helpful thoughts to people who have just experienced a disability, to parents, to pastors, staff and lay people in the church. Each chapter ends with additional questions that push the reader to think more deeply for themselves. While this book doesn't have all the answers—nothing will in this life—it constantly points to scripture and to the One Who does. This is a realistic, but hope-filled book that is worth reading.

Bob Horning, Ph.D. Parent of a child with a disability

David Anderson sounds a wakeup call to the church in his book *Reaching Out and Bringing In*. Built on a solid biblical foundation, the book exhorts the church to follow Jesus's example of compassion and acceptance for all people in need. David reminds us of the misconceptions and misunderstandings that cloud our view and challenges us to see all people through God's eyes. We are called to break down barriers and reach out in new and creative ways to accept and include all people. The book's call for personal heart change is coupled with a challenge to the church to greater action and intentional outreach. You cannot read this book and remain content with the status quo—it will transform the way you view ministry to individuals and families affected by disability in your community.

Vonn Dornbush, D. Min. Pastor of Missions and Outreach, Calvary Church, Roseville, MN

Dr. David Anderson has a burden for disabled persons. I've had the privilege of conducting conferences with him in Eastern Europe and in Africa on ministry to those who are marginalized by disability, disease, or poverty. He is an articulate spokesman for the disabled and the need to include them in any church ministry program.

Dr. Anderson brings years of "on the ground" experience to bear on the issues of a biblical response to disability. He is an effective teacher of both the theology of disability and practical ways to minister to persons who are disabled. His goal, that of mainstreaming disability ministry to "be the same as any other form of ministry: to glorify God through the proclamation of the Gospel, and through living a life that brings honor to the One who has called us to be his children," is the subject of this book. He is practical in his suggestions to open doors to share the Gospel as well as integrate people with disabilities into the life of the church, as a witness to the surrounding community of Christ's love and compassion.

This study can be life-changing for the individual reader and for the Church. Dr. Anderson's passion for inclusion of a ministry to disabled persons as the measure of Christian ministry is clearly and effectively stated. This is a study long overdue.

David W. Johnson, MD. Assistant Clinical Professor of Obstetrics and Gynecology (retired), University of Minnesota Medical School. Short-term medical missionary to Africa, Central America, and Eastern Europe.

After many years of working with individuals and families experiencing disabilities, I thought my understanding and compassion were deep and genuine. *Reaching Out and Bringing In* has challenged my thinking, expanded my heart, and increased my motivation to reach out more to the "largest unreached people group" on the planet—those living with disabilities. This book provides a thorough discussion of the issues that hold us back, speaks truth from God's word to set us free, and gives vision for what God wants to accomplish through us, the body of Christ, both disabled and "temporarily able-bodied" people working together. We need each other, and everyone needs to read this book!

Jody Cowdin, M.A., M.Ed. Executive Director, *The Dwelling Place Shelter,* St Paul, MN

Dr. Anderson's book is well rooted theologically and challenges the church community and her leaders to reach out to people and families affected by disability, and to consider ways the church can minister to and with people with disabilities. The book includes insightful and relevant "For Further Reflection" and "Going Deeper" questions at the end of each chapter making it perfect for reading and discussion by church staff, church boards, and in small group or Sunday School settings.

Brian Funk, Area Director, Joni and Friends Eastern Pennsylvania, Lancaster, PA

Thank you for giving the church and me personally such a wonderful resource to be a better minister of God's grace to our world. May it be true in our churches and homes that our ministry to those with disabilities not be just a job but a part of our calling to be more like Jesus.

Derek Hughes, Family Pastor, Crossroads Bible Church, Bellevue WA

REACHING OUT AND BRINGING IN

Ministry to and with Persons with Disabilities

David W Anderson

WestBow
PRESS
A DIVISION OF THOMAS NELSON

Unless otherwise indicated, all Scripture quotations are from The ESV® Bible (The Holy Bible, English Standard Version®), copyright © 2001 by Crossway. Used by permission. All rights reserved.

Scriptures marked NIV are taken from the Holy Bible, New International Version (NIV). © 1973, 1978, 1984 by International Bible Society. Used by permission of Zondervan Publishing House. All rights reserved.

Scriptures marked MSG are taken from *The Message* by Eugene H. Peterson. © 1993, 1994, 1995, 1996, 2000, 2001, 2002. Used by permission of NavPress Publishing Group.

Scriptures marked NCV are taken from The Holy Bible, New Century Version®. Copyright © 2005 by Thomas Nelson, Inc. Used by permission.

Crossing Bridges, Inc., is an independent, non governmental, inter-denominational, and non profit organization established in 2005 with a mission is to bring light and hope to people with disabilities and their families, around the world. *Crossing Bridges* partners with individuals, families, churches, schools, and other organizations to promote awareness of, and responsiveness to, the needs and abilities of persons facing disabling conditions. We seek to encourage and empower persons dealing with disability—and those who serve them—to bring about changed lives and changed societies. Our goal is to be a catalyst for reconciliation, social justice, and church outreach. This book is a revision and expansion of earlier work printed while serving as a missionary-teacher in Cameroon.

WestBow Press books may be ordered through booksellers or by contacting:

WestBow Press
A Division of Thomas Nelson
1663 Liberty Drive
Bloomington, IN 47403
www.westbowpress.com
1-(866) 928-1240

ISBN: 978-1-4497-9095-0 (sc)
ISBN: 978-1-4908-0555-9 (e)

Library of Congress Control Number: 2013906379

Printed in the United States of America.

WestBow Press rev. date: 8/15/2013

Contents

Foreword

After serving as university professor of special education for twenty-eight years, the last fifteen as director of graduate programs in special education at Bethel University, Dr. Anderson "retired," formed a non-profit called Crossing Bridges, Inc., to create awareness of disability issues, and began ministering on behalf of children and adults with special needs among church leaders in countries like Ukraine, Haiti, Serbia, Ghana, Cameroon, Kenya, and elsewhere.

Wherever David has gone, he has used his skills as a teacher and administrator to serve as an advocate for disabled persons by emphasizing clear biblical teaching and practical application. The contents of this book reveal this same solid commitment to the authority of Scripture and a desire to provide warm, challenging application. Now we all have the privilege of being exposed to the same solid teaching that David has shared in other places.

In addition to providing us with clear insights into key Old Testament and New Testament biblical texts pertaining to issues of disability (e.g., the Book of Job, Isaiah 53, Matthew 9, John 5, James 5, etc.) and addressing pertinent theological issues (e.g., God's sovereignty and suffering, personal sin and disability, healing and the atonement, whether faith is required for a cure, and the dangers of the so-called prosperity gospel, etc.), Dr. Anderson also deals with a wide range of practical issues (e.g., accessibility, cultural misinformation, rampant social injustice, the church's role in providing a loving community, the distinction between people who are "disabled" and those who are "temporarily able-bodied," etc.).

Those of us who identify ourselves as followers of Jesus Christ will again and again appreciate Dr. Anderson's examination of the text of Scripture and his knowledge of such a wide range of theological, ethical and practical issues. And, "Going Deeper" questions at the end of each chapter will promote further reflection. We will also be touched by the personal stories he provides from his years of practical experience. But, hopefully, things won't stop there. For the text of the Bible calls us to action.

Many of us know individuals who are affected by disability. Perhaps that includes you, a family member, or friend. You know firsthand the challenges that often accompany disability. Hopefully, this resource will awaken and equip the Christian community to reach out in practical ways to provide ministries of compassion, while encouraging those dealing directly with the daily care of someone impacted by disability.

Dr. Anderson tells us that his goal in writing is "to help church leaders develop an inclusive worldview that includes persons and families dealing with disabilities, and to challenge churches to intentionally reach out to those individuals and families with the gospel of Jesus Christ and welcome them into Christian fellowship as an integral part of the Body of Christ." Here we will discover ways to apply the Bible in order to serve in Jesus' name those families and individuals in our communities affected by disability, those the author describes as possibly "the largest unreached people group in the world."

As a pastor in the United States for over forty-three years and trainer of church leaders in a several other countries, I found myself challenged by Dr. Anderson's overview of disability, including his treatment of causes and perceptions by society. Even here, the author is thoroughly biblical in reminding us, for example, of the sovereignty of God and that we are all, in some sense, "disabled."

I remember Dr. Anderson telling me that he found it difficult to read passages of the Bible *without* seeing some connection with disability ministry. At the time, I must admit that I thought Dr. Anderson's observation simply reflected his personal passion, nothing more. For this was not my experience. When I examined Scripture, I rarely saw any connection with disability. However, after reading this resource, I now wonder how I could have missed seeing so much, since there is such a wealth of biblical material that deals directly with issues of disability. How could I have missed it? Dr. Anderson's analysis of this topic has challenged me to read the Bible with different eyes.

I only regret, as a pastor, that I wasn't exposed to such clear teaching years ago. I would have been motivated to give more leadership to the kinds of ministries recommended in this book. But it is not too late. I can act now. So can you.

That, really, is the purpose of this book. It *informs* in order to *transform* and promote *action*. The appropriate action for you may differ from the action I intend to take. But we are all called to demonstrate the love of Christ to those affected by disability.

Reaching Out and Bringing In is a workbook that provides rich insights into numerous practical issues related to the care of persons with disabilities and their inclusion in the services of the church. You will be often challenged by statements like this one:

> The Christian Church should be a model for the rest of the world of inclusiveness and accessibility; a place where acceptance and welcome to all people is evident, and where grace is preached and practiced without reservation.

That would be some church, wouldn't it? My prayer is that God would use this practical book to create such church models all over our world. The results would be many: the hurting would receive care, the world would be awakened by the transforming power of the gospel, and God would be glorified!

Dr. Richard C. Schoenert
Pastor Emeritus, Calvary Church, Roseville, MN
Missionary, One Challenge International

Acknowledgments

There are probably more people that I can name who have contributed to this work in one way or another, people whose teaching, writing, and lives have been used by God to shape me into the person I am—even though some may not be aware. Certainly, I must acknowledge my wife, Florence, for the years of support and encouragement she has given and is; and our daughters, Jennifer, Melissa, and Amy, along with the eight grandchildren God has blessed us with.

I appreciate those who reviewed the manuscript and chose to write an endorsement to the work—Jody Cowdin, Dana Croxton, Vonn Dornbush, Brian Funk, Don Mortenson, Derek Hughes, David Johnson, and Bob Horning, who also provided valuable editorial comments on the manuscript. Some have been professional colleagues, others are people I have ministered with in various Joni and Friends activities, and one is the parent of a daughter with a disability. My association and conversations with each have in some way contributed to the ideas expressed in this book.

Dr. Richard Schoenert deserves special mention. Having served as my pastor for a number of years, he has added significantly to my spiritual development and understanding of Scripture. His spiritual influence goes beyond his pastoral leadership; his friendship and encouragement continue to be important as my journey with God moves forward. Both of us received a call to missions after years of other service to the Lord; I am grateful for the opportunities to minister with him in Ukraine and Haiti.

During the academic year 2002–2003, I taught at Good News Theological College and Seminary (GNTCS) in Ghana. Knowing of my involvement in disability issues, Dr. Thomas Oruro, president of GNTCS, requested that I develop and teach a course to make the students aware of the need and opportunity to minister to people affected by disability. That course was groundwork for this book.

I must also thank all the people with disabilities that God has brought across my path, especially the children in Cameroon at the Center for Empowerment of Females with Disabilities (CEFED) for what they have taught me. It has been my privilege to work with Nungu Magdalene Manyi, the Director of CEFED, to help church leaders understand the importance of reaching out to persons with disabilities. The families affected by disability that I have met in Serbia, Romania, Cameroon and Ghana at Family Retreats, in sharing their struggles and their joys, have also contributed to this book.

Most of all, I want to acknowledge God for his grace expressed to me in various ways each day. He has been leading me on a fascinating journey as a husband, father, special education teacher, university professor, missionary-teacher, and has given me various roles to fill in his church—all the while helping me to understand more about who he is and who I am as his child and servant. And the individuals with disabilities he has brought across my path are among my greatest teachers.

Introduction:

Reflection on
Matthew 9:35–38

Imagine Jesus traveling with his disciples, ministering to the spiritual and physical needs of people. As he scans the horizon, he sees crowds approaching—many perhaps with obvious infirmities, all with deep spiritual needs. As his heart overflows with compassion he draws an analogy between this disorganized mass of people and the fields around him that are ready to be harvested. His words convey intense compassion toward people who are distressed, discouraged, disenfranchised—thrown down, cast off, driven away, without care and attention, even by the spiritual leaders of Israel. They are like sheep without a shepherd—pushed aside, to the margins of society.

Undoubtedly, the persons Jesus encountered were those to whom he referred when he announced his mission in the synagogue of Nazareth:

> The Spirit of the Lord . . . has anointed me to proclaim good news to the poor. He has sent me to proclaim liberty to the captives and recovering of sight to the blind, to set at liberty those who are oppressed, to proclaim the year of the Lord's favor. (Luke 4:18–19)

Many of those who came seeking Jesus may have been physically exhausted, fatigued from the hardship of daily life, and perhaps troubled by an awareness of their sinfulness. Others may have been weakened by disease or infirmity, burdened by oppression from those in positions of power or authority. Today, we would refer to such people as *marginalized,* assigned a place at the outer edges of society, hidden from view.

Compassion for the oppressed such as Jesus expressed calls for a response from his followers— one of bringing comfort, lightening their load, seeking justice for the poor, and upholding the cause of those in need (cf. Psalm 140:12). Jesus spoke emphatically in urging that prayer be made to the Lord of the harvest to *thrust* or *throw forth* (Greek: *ekballo*; to expel, eject, drive or cast out) laborers to get the job done.

The image of crops ready for harvesting points to the pressing need to gather the fruit of the land before it is lost—the harvest is, after all, of great value to the one who owns the field and to those who will share in its bounty. But in Jesus's illustration, the Lord of the harvest is God, and the harvest is humankind made in the image of the Creator; hence, the value is enormous and eternal.

Most often when Matthew 9:35–38 is quoted, it is given as a challenge for believers to engage in missionary or evangelistic activity, the focus being on the need for *workers*. But for our purposes,

I want to center on the *harvest*. As the Good Shepherd, Jesus challenges us not only to pray, but to respond to the call for workers to bring in the harvest. In the context of this workbook, the point is that a significant part of this harvest has been neglected by the Church: individuals and families who are affected by disability. My goal is to help church leaders develop an inclusive worldview that includes persons and families dealing with disabilities, and to challenge churches to intentionally reach out to these individuals and families with the gospel of Jesus Christ and welcome them into Christian fellowship as integral parts of the Body of Christ.

Challenge or Opportunity?

The population of the world is estimated to be more than 7 billion persons (as of November 2012). The standard used by the World Health Organization (2012) and other international organizations to estimate the number of people with disabilities is 15%. This means there are 1.05 billion persons with disabilities worldwide. Approximately 80% of these are thought to live in developing nations. When we add to this statistic the number of family members whose lives are impacted by having a disabled family member, it becomes clear that this "harvest" is a significant number of persons—a group that would comprise the largest country in the world, surpassing China or India in population! And, given that the Church has generally overlooked this group, we recognize that they form *the largest unreached people group in the world*. Technically, from a missiological point of view, an unreached people group refers to homogeneous people sharing a common language and sense of ethnic identity, history, and customs, within which there are no indigenous Christian churches or in which less than 2% of the population are Christ-followers. In this technical sense, people with disabilities are not a single people group. But people with disabilities are the largest unreached group of people, representing every race and culture. They are unreached in many parts of the world because of cultural and traditional (mis) understandings of disability, as will be discussed in chapter two. And even in Western nations, the majority of churches have yet to engage in any intentional outreach and ministry to and with disabled individuals. Bill Amstutz, President of Shepherds Ministries (Union Grove, WI), made this point regarding the church and people with disabilities:

> We can get people with disabilities into the building. We have ramps, we have extra parking—we have all kinds of things for that. But the attitude of receptivity and making sure that they are reached with the Gospel has been a little slower. (*Mission Network News*, 2011)

The Church's Response

How should the Church respond to these statistics? To focus only on the enormity of this group would lead many Christians to feel overwhelmed by a sense of helplessness, perhaps leading to despair and their continuing to ignore individuals and families so affected. Some may respond that they have no one with a disability in their church. To them, I would ask two questions: *"Are you sure?"* and *"Why is there no one in your church who has a disability?"* The next chapter will address the first question by raising the issue of hidden disabilities and weaknesses that the onlooker may be unaware of. To the second question, I would further inquire whether this absence of persons with disability in the church is because of a lack of outreach (intentional or unintentional), or because the church is not welcoming or accessible. Some may view persons who are disabled as unworthy and choose to ignore them; still others, out of ignorance about or fear of disability, may treat them with contempt or judgment.

The Scarcity Paradigm

Brett Webb-Mitchell (1994b) used the term *scarcity paradigm* to explain why people question the wisdom of spending time and money on individuals with severe disabilities when the effort and resources might better be used to solve "real" problems faced by the church or society. A church that operates with a minimal budget may take the position that income (tithes and offerings) and other valued resources are limited or scarce. These limited resources may be considered neither renewable nor expendable, requiring that they be used cautiously and in a way that will bring wide benefit. Such a view frames persons with disabilities negatively, suggesting that people with disabilities will create a drain on already limited time, money, staff, and resources, and may be unable to contribute (financially or otherwise) to advance the church. Or, based on unbiblical understanding of disability, some may believe that a person who is or becomes disabled "got what they deserved" because of sin. Thus, questions are asked as to the value of serving persons who are disabled, particularly those with severe impairments. Such thoughts suggest an underlying *negative* valuation not only of ministry to persons with disabilities, but of those individuals themselves: "Why spend scarce resources on persons who will never bring benefit to the church in return?" This reasoning fosters a Darwinian-like attitude in which the 'fittest' are favored to receive the benefit.

Though not dealing specifically with disability, the scarcity paradigm seems at play in the account of Jesus's feeding the 5000 (John 6:1–14; cf. Matthew 14:15–20; Mark 6:30–44; Luke 9:10–17). Jesus and his disciples had sought to be alone on the mountainside—perhaps a time to debrief and refresh themselves. Jesus is seated with his disciples when the approaching crowds are spotted. Again, Matthew (9:14) and Mark (6:34) comment on Jesus being moved with compassion for the people, and responding by curing some who were diseased or disabled and teaching them many things. As time passes Jesus raises the issue of food: "Where are we to buy bread, so that these people may eat?" His intent is to test (Greek: *pierazo*) the disciples—to examine or assess their faith by putting them in a position where their faith would be stretched. The word *test* is neutral, meaning the question was asked as a means of training the disciples by challenging them with responsibility. Jesus knew the difficulty this would entail (as far as the disciples's ability to solve the problem), and already knew how he would meet the need. That Jesus specifically asked Philip where food could be purchased was probably because Philip was from Bethsaida (John 1:14), which was relatively close to where they were. Some biblical scholars have suggested that Philip was the disciple charged with procuring supplies (just as Judas was in charge of the money box, John 13:29), making it logical that Jesus would single him out to ask about obtaining food for the crowd.

The question caused Philip to try to come up with a "human" solution, though Jesus knew there was none. Jesus's question was *where* bread could be purchased, but Philip's answer centered more on *how*, focusing on the cost of buying food for so many and the limited resources of the disciples. According to Bruce Milne (1993), they would have needed earnings equivalent of eight months of labor. Andrew responded by bringing to Jesus a young child who had in his lunch box five small rolls or scones and two fish, probably pickled fish used as relish, in the same way as sardines are used today as hors d'oeuvres (Tenny, 1953, p. 112). But Andrew does not seem hopeful and asks "What are they for so many?"

In similar fashion, given the large number of people and families affected by disability in the world, the scarcity paradigm causes many churches to ask "What are *we* for so many?" The answer, of course, lies in what God is able to do or accomplish through those who are willing to follow the example of our Lord in showing compassion to the "many." God does not expect any *one* of us, or any *one* church, to minister to the hundreds of millions of persons with disabilities. But we are all capable of ministering to those present in our community. And, as with the meager contents of the young boy's lunch pail, God can do much with the little we possess—or with the little we think we have to offer personally.

A More Appropriate Response

I suggest that a more appropriate response is for the Church to recognize the presence of individuals and families affected by disability in their community as a pivotal opportunity to model the practice of Christian love and to obey Christ's command to preach the Gospel to every creature (Mark 16:15). As with the disciples in John 6, Jesus may be seeking to stretch our faith and confidence in him, or to reveal to us something new about him, when he presents us with various challenges—in the context of this book, the challenge of interacting with persons and families affected by disability. We need to live by (in) faith, expecting to see God work, and blessing to abound both to those with whom he asks us to minister and to ourselves. Jesus has given us, his present-day disciples, the responsibility and the authority to minister to all people groups in his name (Matthew 28:18–20). We must not limit God's ability or desire to work *in us* and *though us* to bring glory to himself.

Though we may have limited resources, Warren Wiersbe's comment on the feeding of the 5000 can apply to us as we minister to persons affected with disability: "The practical lesson is clear: whenever there is a need, give all that you have to Jesus and let Him do the rest. Begin with what you have, but be sure you give it all to Him" (Wiersbe, 2001a). What we, as individuals or as a church, have to offer may be limited—like the five small rolls and two small fish—but A. W. Pink pointed to what God is able to do with these small offerings as we make them (and ourselves) available to him:

> [Christ] did not scorn the loaves because they were few in number, nor the fish either because they were 'small.' *This tells us that God is pleased to use small and weak things.* He used the tear of a babe to move the heart of Pharaoh's daughter. He used the shepherd-rod of Moses to work mighty miracles in Egypt. He used David's sling and stone to overthrow the Philistine giant. He used a 'little maid' to bring the mighty Naaman to Elisha. He used a widow with a handful of meal to sustain His prophet. He used a 'little child' to teach His disciples a much needed lesson in humility. So here, He uses the five loaves and two small fishes to feed this great multitude....But mark it carefully, it was only as these loaves and fishes were placed in the *hands of Christ* that they were made efficient and sufficient. (Pink, 1975, pp. 296–297, emphasis added)

Not only does this cause us to focus on how God is able to use what we have (or are) to accomplish much, but it also causes us to recognize our assumption that people with disabilities have little to offer may be incorrect. Often people who are able-bodied view persons with disabilities as "small and weak things"—people who are insignificant, not worthy of attention, unable to contribute in any beneficial manner. Pink reminds us that God's intentions are often carried out through his use of weakness so that the glory goes to him, not to the actor he employs.

The Focus of this Book

"The harvest is plentiful," said Jesus, "but the workers are few; ask the Lord of the harvest to send out workers into his harvest field" (Matthew 9:37–38). How can your church become "harvesters" among those whom society, both civil and religious, has neglected for so long?

Most churches do not have persons with obvious disabilities in their congregation—except, perhaps, for older adults who have been a part of the church for many years but, because of age, have limited hearing or visual ability, or children of the church "fathers" who have a disability. And most church leaders do not feel prepared to minister with persons affected by disability or their families. Yet the church has been commissioned by the Lord Jesus Christ to bring the gospel to *all* people groups (Matthew 28:18–20). This requires reaching out to, welcoming, and including those affected by disability into the community of faith. Church leaders must have—and teach—a biblical view of disability, persons who have a disability, and the church's role in ministering to these individuals and their families. What is presented in this book will help develop such a biblical view. It can be used as a workbook for independent study or to accompany a seminar or conference designed to create awareness among church leaders of the opportunities and challenges presented by the presence of persons with disabilities in the local and global community, and to develop basic knowledge and skill to engage in ministry to and alongside persons with disabilities.

Several issues related to disability will be explored, with the intent to tear down barriers that have been erected between people with and without disabilities, and discover ways the Church can minister to and with persons who have a disability. Chapter one will provide a general introduction to the world of disability. Chapter two explores human barriers that impinge on people with disabilities and their families, as well as introducing God's view of disability and people with disabilities. In chapters three and four we will explore biblical/theological themes which inform and give direction to churches and individuals who engage in disability ministry. Without a proper understanding of these Scriptural principles, churches will be unmotivated to intentionally reach out to persons and families affected by disability. For some, this may be a review of theological concepts already known, but since most Bible schools and seminaries do not specifically address disability issues, this study may lead to new insights. Chapters five and six delve into practical aspects of disability ministry, with particular emphasis on understanding and ministering to families affected by disability. Chapter seven looks at issues of health and healing related to disability, and chapter eight addresses disability and the problem of evil and suffering from a theological/philosophical perspective.

Wherever I have shared these topics with church leaders, their response has been repentance of their oversight and a commitment to follow Jesus's example of ministry to marginalized and ignored people. My prayer is that all who read this book will search the Scriptures for themselves and, as they study and complete the "exercises" that accompany each chapter, will by moved by God's Spirit to intentionally reach out to persons and families affected by disability, either individually or through their churches.

Going Deeper

Introductory questions:

1. Using the 15% figure, what is the estimated number of disabled persons in your country?

2. Is there anyone in your church with a disability? If not, why do you think this is the case?

3. Do you personally know someone with a disability, or a family affected by disability?

4. How comfortable would you be if someone with a disability joined your congregation?

5. Have you considered that at some point in your life *you* might become disabled?

6. How prepared do you feel, not only to *welcome* someone with a disability, but to *minister* to and with that individual?

A closer look at John 6:1–14

1. What did Jesus "see" when the crowds approached? What did the disciples "see"?

2. Why were the people coming to Jesus? What were they seeking in coming to Jesus?

3. How did Philip view the problem?

4. How did Andrew respond to the situation?

5. What might the young boy with his lunch box "see"?

6. What or how can you contribute to ministry with persons who have disabilities?

Section One
Fundamentals of Disability

Chapter One

Basic Concepts About Disability

The Man with a Disability—John 5

John 5 tells the story of Jesus's encounter with a man lying in the portico of the Pool of Bethesda who has been disabled for 38 years. A look as this familiar passage from the perspective of disability will help us gain new perspective.

> After this there was a feast of the Jews, and Jesus went up to Jerusalem. Now there is in Jerusalem by the Sheep Gate a pool, in Aramaic called Bethesda, which has five roofed colonnades. In these lay a multitude of invalids—blind, lame, and paralyzed. One man was there who had been an invalid for thirty-eight years. When Jesus saw him lying there and knew that he had already been there a long time, he said to him, "Do you want to be healed?" (John 5:1–6)

Inquisitive minds wish John provided more details about the man's condition. John uses the Greek word *asthenia*, which means weakness, infirmity, or disease. Astheneia, or weakness, carries the idea of being without strength, incapacitated in some serious way (Richards, 1999, p. 621). Several versions of the Bible translate astheneia as *illness*. In biblical times, much less was known about human anatomy and the specifics of various disabilities, resulting in terminology being less diversified than today. Hence, disability and disease were not differentiated. Even terms which we might think are more telling—blind, deaf, lame, and mute, for example—lack the specificity of today's understanding of disability.

Given the fact that the man is not able to move into the pool without assistance, we can understand his physical impairment to be severe. John does not tell us the specific nature of the man's disability, nor whether the man has been in this condition since birth or became disabled as the result of an illness or accident. If his disability was not from birth, we wonder how old the man was when Jesus met him. How many of those 38 years of impairment were spent by the Pool of Bethesda? These details are not provided because they are not necessary to John's purpose that his readers may "believe that Jesus is the Christ, the Son of God, and that by believing [they] may have life in his name" (John 20:31). In fact, John's focus is not so much on the miracle itself but the ensuing controversy between Jesus and the Jewish religious leaders, a controversy which leads them to determine to get rid of Jesus (John 5:18). Characteristic of John's gospel, the curing of the man is not referred to as a "*miraculous work*," emphasizing God's power (*dunamis*), but as a "*sign*" (*semeion*) confirming that Jesus is the Son of God and has a God-given commission to bring life in all its fullness (John 10:10).

The story of this man underscores how people with disabilities or certain diseases are pushed aside by the more powerful, able-bodied members of the civil or the religious society. There is an ironic element to Jesus's encounter with the man—the man is found lying by the Pool of Bethesda, which means *house of kindness or mercy*. But this was something which the man apparently could not count on from his countrymen. We are told that he has been by the pool for perhaps all of those 38 years. Oddly, he is not completely discouraged—perhaps thinking that given opportune conditions he *could* be the first to enter the water and be cured—but he recognizes that without the help of another, this will not happen. You get a sense of his loneliness and near-hopelessness when, in response to Jesus's asking if he wanted to be cured of his disability, the man does not give a direct answer ("yes" or "no"), but replies "I have no one to put me into the pool when the water is stirred up" (John 5:7).

According to tradition, when the waters of the pool were "stirred" by the angel of the Lord, the first person to enter would be cured of disability or disease (cf. John 5:3–4, KJV). But the man's hope of being the first into the waters is weak. Many people with disabilities were probably at the pool each day, all with the same intent: to be first into the water when stirred by the angel and be cured. It is not known how often this moving of the waters occurred (or when it had last occurred), but the man was aware of the fact that having no one to assist him, others who were diseased, blind, deaf, or less physically impaired could enter the water more quickly. Perhaps at some earlier time, he had family who would bring him to the pool. But over the years, even they had grown weary and abandoned him. Apparently he had no friends available, nor could he expect any compassion from other, able-bodied persons who would surely know of his presence at the pool because of his long history of begging.

It appears that the man is not only physically paralyzed, but also emotionally paralyzed (Milne, 1993). His response to Jesus's question seems to be one of despair, perhaps mingled with anger that no one was present (willing?) to assist him into the pool should the water be stirred (which would require someone to be with him continuously). Bruce Milne suggested that the man remains locked inside his own need and the belief that the only way he could be cured was through entering the pool at the right moment. As John recounts the story, there is no indication the man had any expectation that Jesus was able to cure him of his disability. In fact, he appears to know nothing of Jesus, perhaps because this occurred early in Jesus's ministry or because of his situation.

For those around him and for the man himself, being disabled had become a descriptor of *who* he was. The "invalid" (as astheneia is translated in the ESV and NIV) was the sum of his identity, the way he was seen and known by those who passed by as he waited by the Pool of Bethesda. To be cured of his disability—something which he has lived with for 38 years—would have significant implications for his whole concept of life and how he understood the world and himself. If his infirmity prevented him from sitting or standing, his entire view of the world would be from a position of lying on his mat, thus altering his concept of spatial relations and spatial orientation. Those able to sit and stand without difficulty cannot imagine what life would be like for someone so paralyzed. Additionally, the man may spend his days and nights in that same spot beside the Pool of Bethesda. Having become accustomed to such a limited lifestyle, he would have no real hopes or dreams of a future that moved beyond the confines of the portico by the pool. Vocational options were limited by his condition, which would have "equipped" him only to beg for money.

The man's response to Jesus suggests that he had accepted this identity as a disabled man. It is probable that his self-concept was as dim as his personal aspirations. This is key to our focus: The man's condition did not affect only his mobility; it resulted in his being cut off from human relationships—he had no one to help him. Yet it was not *his condition* that brought about his loneliness and isolation, but the *attitude of the able-bodied toward him* in his condition. Notice that after being cured by Jesus, when the man is challenged by the Jewish religious leaders, they do not react to his new physical ability, only to the fact that he was in violation of the Sabbath law by carrying his mat (John 5:10). (Technically, this was not a violation of the Old Testament law which focused on doing a normal day's work on the Sabbath. Rather, he was transgressing the traditions which the Pharisees had added to "explain" the law.) The attitude of the Jewish leaders toward the man seems unaffected by his cure. Very likely they had considered his physical disability a sign that he was a sinner (the typical view of the Jews, as seen in the Book of Job). For him now to break the Sabbath tradition both confirmed their opinion and affirmed them in their judgment.

More will be said about this attitude later. For now, the story of Jesus's encounter with the man serves as a backdrop against which to introduce some basic concepts necessary to understand disability.

Human Variation

The Bible is clear in teaching that God is the Creator of all that is (Genesis 1–2; Colossians 1:16–17; Hebrews 1:2, 11:1–3), and makes it evident that uniformity is *not* the goal of creation. Genesis 1:1–2 tells us that God created the heavens and the earth but they were "without form and void" (Hebrew: *tohu* and *bohu*). Out of this initial "chaos" God acted to display his creative imagination and artistry (Genesis 1:3–27, 2:7) in what Wiersbe explained as a pattern of *forming* and *filling*:

> He made three spheres of activity: the heavens, the landmasses, and the waters; and then He filled them with appropriate forms of life . . . . God has now created three special "spaces": the land, the seas, and the expanse of the sky. During the next three creative days, He will fill these spaces. (Wiersbe, 2001c)

Plantinga regarded creation as "an act of imaginative love" (Plantinga, 2002, p. 23) as God designed and created an hospitable environment for the highest of his creation, humankind. There is tremendous variety in all that God created, both in the visible realm and "hidden" within creation for humankind to discover as they explore, develop, and care for God's world. Wiersbe considered creation a wordless book declaring God's power and creativity (cf. Psalm 19:1–4) (Wiersbe, 2004). All that God created on earth and in the expanse of the universe attests to, but does not exhaust his glory nor capture its entirety. "From the uniqueness of each snowflake to the individuality shown in the animal world, God's delight in creative expression and His concern for individuals are shown" (Richards, 1987, Genesis 1).

Genesis 1:31 records God's assessment of his creative activity: "God saw everything that he had made, and behold, it was very good." A few verses later, we read "on the seventh day God finished his work that he had done, and he rested on the seventh day from all his work that he had done" (Genesis 2:2). The words suggest that God was both pleased and satisfied with his creative handiwork. We can assume that during the time between God's completion of creation and the events of Genesis 3 (the temptation and fall), there was no disease or disability. Although God created a world in which there was the *potential* for evil (humankind was free to choose to love and obey God or to move away from God through disobedience) and the *potential* for disability, these were not realized until Eve succumbed to the serpent's enticement and Adam willfully chose to disobey God's command not to eat of the fruit of the tree of knowledge of good and evil. However, impairment and disability were not present in the world as God originally intended. But we can still assume that there would be diversity beyond simply the male/female distinction. Psalm 139:13–16 describes God's involvement in the creation of each individual, knitting us together according to his design, including our physicality and our abilities. Personal differences, including strengths and limitations are a part of the diversity of God's creation; we all have things at which we are good and things at which we are not so good. Each of us is different from the other in various ways, some visible (such as gender, age, height, weight, skin or eye color, race or ethnicity) and some less obvious (such as academic achievement, talents, interests, motor and athletic ability, or intelligence). Variation among all God's creation is as God planned. God did not create everyone the same: "Each of us is unrepeatable, a unique bearer and reflector of the glory of God" (Plantinga, 2002, p. 40).

We need to recognize that *difference is normal.* God did not create everyone exactly the same, as if produced on an assembly line like automobiles and electronic equipment where sameness is important. The vast diversity within God's creation leads to the conclusion that *God loves variety.* Even individuals within the same immediate family are just that—individuals. Despite surface resemblances, each has her or his own strengths and weaknesses, personality traits, talents, and interests. This suggests that God is bored with 'sameness.' One thing all humans have in common, however, is vulnerability to events that are beyond our control, including accidents and illnesses that could result in a disability.

What is "Normal"?

We can say, then, that prior to the events of Genesis 3, the absence of disease and disability was normal, but since the fall of humankind *that* normal no longer exists. Things changed: childbirth now involves pain and the marital relationship is altered (Genesis 3:16), and work now involves pain and effort (Genesis 3:17–19). Creation itself was cursed—subjected to futility and in bondage to corruption (Romans 8:20–21). As a result, neither humankind nor the sub-human creation are able to conform to God's original intent apart from God's intervention. Paul said we groan and all creation groans as we await the consummation. In other words, when Adam and Eve put their own interests ahead of obedience to God's command, the world became *abnormal.* Disability is now a normal part of life because we live in an abnormal world—sin has significantly altered what God had intended. Disability and disease are part of our sin-filled world, and are a constant reminder that all is not right with the world.

> For the first time, brokenness and difficulty were introduced. This marring of creation permeated not only the spiritual, but also the physical, the intellectual, the emotional, the psychological, and the social. The effects continue to carry over today into our work, our world, our bodies, and our relationships with self, others, and God. (Hubach, 2006, p. 28).

The Tyranny of "Normalcy"

Normal is often defined as the absence of deviance, illness, or disability, making it a definition of exclusion—if those characteristics are not present in a person, he or she is judged to be "normal" (Smart, 2001). In this technical sense, "normal" carries no value judgment as to goodness or badness; valuation (positive or negative) is something which individuals add based on their own circumstances, preferences, or biases. A major problem with the concept of normalcy is that people tend to equate *normal* with *natural* and *abnormal* with *unnatural*. This strongly influences their thinking upon encountering someone who is different, whether that difference is because of disability, ethnicity, or any other factor external to the person's "being." Because of unfamiliarity with disability and lack of association with persons who are disabled, the response of many is fear and avoidance, resulting in conscious or unconscious discrimination. Rather than taking time to get to know a person with a disability as an individual, people tend to stereotype her or him based on limited and often inaccurate information about both the disability and the individual.

Statistically speaking, *normal* refers to *average* or *typical*. "Average" pertains to the range in which approximately 50% of the population falls on standardized tests of intellectual or academic ability, or physical growth patterns. The world, however, is comprised of an additional 50% whose scores fall above or below the relatively narrow average range. My point is that the presence of diversity and difference in our now abnormal world *is* typical, or "normal." To describe as normal only those who are of average ability, average achievement, average height or weight, average looks, or even average age creates an artificial and unreal picture of the world. We each possess inherent strengths and weaknesses. Since we are all distinctly created by God, *normal* becomes a meaningless concept: "To talk of people being 'normal or deviating from the normal' is not consistent with Christian teaching. It is to undermine the essential uniqueness of every individual" (Harrison, 1995, p. 26). People do not deviate *from* normal; deviation *is* normal. Differences are to be expected and, because both humankind (regardless of ability or disability) and the rest of creation are under the curse, disability is to be expected. "But God in his wisdom has made it so that we 'normal' people have a lot to gain not only from serving persons with disabilities, but also in being served by them or in learning from them."[1]

Hauerwas (2004) commented that "The demand to be normal can be tyrannical unless we understand that the normal condition of our being together is that we are all different" (p. 40). Speaking specifically in reference to persons with intellectual impairments, Hauerwas held that recognizing our differences enables us all to flourish as different people. In contrast, human (sinful) pride causes people to elevate themselves above others who display a significant weakness that society labels as disability. Focus then falls on the impairment rather than the individual, blinding us to the humanity of the person and causing us to miss that person's potential and beauty as someone created in the image of God—as well as to recognize that he or she is also a sinner in need of God's grace. To see the person behind the disability, our notion of "people" (normal, or ideal) must draw exemplars from a range spanning from severely disabled to highly

---

[1]   Bob Horning, personal communication, February 25, 2013.

gifted persons (cf. Patterson, 1998, p. 136ff). I have included at the end of this book several books written by or about people with disabilities which can help provide such exemplars.

Walter Wink (1995), formerly a professor of biblical interpretation at Auburn Theological Seminary, used his own experience to illustrate how we often meet people we assume to be non disabled but who, in fact, have various invisible conditions or problems that limit their functioning. His various physical ailments (toe deformity, chronic back pain, irregular heartbeat, and hyperglycemia), though not as limiting as some physical disabilities, were health impairments that interfered with his ability to participate fully in some common activities of daily life. Because he had the appearance of being "normal" he was not subject to the ostracism or isolation frequently experienced by more visibly disabled persons (such as the man in John 5). Wink held that the problem is not with those who have a disability, but with the idea of *normalcy* itself, which he understood to be the basis from which mistreatment of people with disabilities originates: "The idea of normalcy . . . is a pathological notion that creates illness, persecution, and the rejection of our God-given uniqueness" (Wink, p. 11). The effect of this faulty understanding of normalcy may be the root cause of how the man in John 5 perceived himself and was treated by those around him.

Only Two Kinds of People

For now, we can say that in reality there are only two kinds of people: those who are *disabled* and those who are *temporarily able-bodied*. This second group is considered *temporarily* able-bodied because anyone can have an accident, develop a serious illness, or become the victim of violence that could bring about a physical or sensory impairment. Additionally, as we age, the possibility of becoming physically impaired or losing some or all of our ability to hear or see increases simply because our bodies wear out. And, following Wink's reasoning, even temporarily able-bodied persons exist on a continuum from those with very mild impairments or limitations to those who are fully able.

To focus heavily on a person's disability obscures the *person*. We see the impairment, the limitation, the absence of function, and wrongly conclude that the *person* is flawed or impaired, sinful or cursed. It is important to remember that beneath the disability is a person who, just as those who are temporarily able-bodied, is created in the image of God. We must also recognize that even persons with severe and multiple impairments are more *like* than *un*like persons without a disability. Just as the temporarily able-bodied have social, emotional, and spiritual needs and longings, so do persons with disabilities. And, just as with temporarily able-bodied persons, persons with a disability also have abilities that may go unrecognized. Differences related to the disability must be respected, but similarities between persons with and without disabilities also must be acknowledged and appreciated. The disability is only one characteristic of the person. The tendency to focus solely on what the person cannot do must be resisted so that we recognize what the person is able to do, and honor who the person *is*. Cultures tend to judge people based on outward characteristics—such as beauty, intelligence, talent, strength, productivity, wealth, and ability. As Christians, our vision needs to be like that of God, who does not look on outward appearances (1 Samuel 16:7); we need to see others as God does (cf. Deuteronomy 1:17, 16:19; Romans 2:11).

What Disability *is* and *is Not*

"Disability" is an ambiguous term used to describe a number of specific conditions which vary both in the aspects of functioning affected and in the degree of limitation, ranging from mild to severe and profound. Simply understood, disability refers to a physical, sensory, or mental impairment which substantially limits one or more major life activities, such as education, employment, or the ability to move about freely in society. However, limitations on the individual's ability to receive an education, be employed, or participate in socially-valued activities (such as going to church) can also result from people's negative attitudes toward or misperception of disability—or of the individual with a disability—or simply from society's neglect of persons with significant needs. It is important to recognize that disability does not define the person; it does not speak to who that person is or what that person may be capable of accomplishing in and through his or her life. Rather than being something a person *is,* a disability is something the person *has.*

The natural, though sinful, tendency is to push away those perceived as different; to devalue them or consider them less worthy or unworthy. It is often assumed that a person with a disability will be unproductive, always taking but never giving to society. Given that expectation, it is unlikely that the person with the disability will have an opportunity to disprove that prejudgment. But *less able* does not mean *less worthy.* Disability does not mean the person is incomplete, powerless, or in need of pity. It does not mean the person is sick (though disability may be a result of serious illness, it is a condition, not a disease). Nor does it mean that the person has *all* the disabilities; having one aspect of functioning affected does not mean all areas are affected. And having a disability does not necessarily mean the person is suffering (except from the prejudicial, degrading attitudes of temporarily able-bodied persons). Theologian Thomas Reynolds asserted that "Full personhood is neither diminished by disability nor confirmed by ability" (2008, p. 42).

Terminology of Disability

The account of Jesus and the man who had a disability in John 5 illustrates the problem of language as applied to persons with disabilities, and how language can cause us to think a certain way. I have already referred to John's use of the word *astheneia* as a descriptor of the man (John 5:5). The meaning of this word includes infirmity (as it is translated in the King James Version), feebleness, impotence, and weakness. However, in the NIV and ESV, the word is translated "invalid." Technically, this English word indicates a person who is weak or disabled by illness or injury. But invalid can also mean being without foundation or having no importance. Understood this way, the term would suggest that the person is *in-valid,* that is, without validity or value. This corresponds to the unfavorable and destructive understanding of disability described above. Although a lack of validity may not be in mind when the person is referred to as an invalid, the subtle negativity implied may alter the way in which the person is perceived and valued by society, or even the individual's self-perception. Indeed, in many cultures today children born with a disabling condition—or diagnosed prenatally as potentially having a disabling condition (such as Down's Syndrome)—are considered "throw-away" babies, and are aborted, allowed to die after birth through starvation or exposure to the elements, given up for adoption, or simply abandoned. Often, a person who becomes disabled through accident, illness, or violence is perceived as no longer being of any worth and may unnecessarily be relieved of job responsibilities or similarly abandoned by the family. Amie, for example, a young mother in Cameroon, had a mild stroke when delivering her fourth child. The infant was unharmed, but Amie was left with a slight physical disability. Her husband took her to a local shaman who, through physical and sexual abuse, attempted to "cure" the disability. When his efforts to bring about a cure failed, Amie's husband kept the children but renounced Amie, casting her aside.

Sociological "Disability"

Not all languages make a clear distinction between the words *impairment, disability,* and *handicap.* Technically, *impairment* refers to the actual condition, such as cerebral palsy, detached retina, or spinal cord injury. Impairments are problems of bodily function or structure. *Disability* signifies the functional limitations in activity or ability to participate in various life activities. Despite these technical differences in meaning, however, impairment and disability are often used interchangeably.

When speaking more directly of an individual's condition, it is appropriate to refer to the impairment (the actual problem) or the disability (the functional limitation). But in recent years there has been an attempt to move from a medically-based understanding of disability to a sociological conceptualization. The sociological concept of "disability" is somewhat elusive, and can even be misleading because it incorporates value judgments by others. *Disability* becomes a social-cultural category that is understood on a continuum—a matter of *more or less* rather than *yes or no.* Conceptually, it does not refer to the individual's physical or mental condition alone but includes the contribution of the environmental and cultural milieu (World Health Organization, 2011, p. 5). Just as one's understanding of "beauty" is personally or culturally determined, disability includes personal and cultural value judgments as well. These cultural overtones often have negative connotations, based on the bias of the majority population (i.e., the temporarily able-bodied).

The intent of the sociological view is to call greater attention to environmental and attitudinal responses to disability. For temporarily able-bodied persons, disability is generally associated with personal incapacity and is often accompanied by negative images and attitudes based on stereotype, lack of accurate information, and lack of relationship with someone who has a physical or mental impairment. Supporters of the sociological view stress the impact of the individual's physical, social, and relational environment on the person's experience of disability.

This argument has some validity, but in effect, it downplays the person's functional limitation caused by the impairment. It assigns to the word *disability* the same negativity that became attached to the word *handicapped* in the 1980s, suggesting that the only problem is that the environment (including services that are or are not available to the person) creates disability, not the actual impairment. This makes disability something which "arises out of a situation in which we are, and *not* a condition which is in us" (Peter, 2011, p. 71). This broadens the category of disability to include whatever a particular group defines it to be: "every disabling condition is a cultural invention or social construction rather than a personal or private problem" (Webb-Mitchell, 1996, p. 126). Disability, then can be descriptive of anyone. Everyone—disabled or temporarily able-bodied—deals with some limitations ("disability") depending on the situation. In this sense, *disability,* like *handicap,* becomes a subjective term used, not to refer to the individual, but to a situation or circumstance that creates a barrier for the person with the impairment—such as a long staircase which a person in a wheelchair cannot negotiate, perhaps even with assistance.

While the response of the physical and social environment does contribute to the impairment's effect on the individual and the family affected by disability—such as limited or inaccessible buildings or programs, absence of necessary accommodations or modifications, or obvious neglect or exclusion—we must still recognize that the physical or mental impairment also limits the person's ability to participate freely in the community. The young girl I met in Ghana, for example, who was born without eyes (skin covered her face where eyes should have been), is not disabled simply because of her environment; she is blind. In the same way, it was not just the isolation and neglect he experienced, nor the architecture of the portico by the pool of Bethesda that caused the man in John 5 to be disabled; it was his paralysis. Nonetheless, the sociological view does give some instruction as to the role the church can play in responding to people who are disabled.

Typical Causes and Correlates of Disability

The history of the treatment of persons with disabilities has been one of ignorance and isolation. When a person becomes disabled or gives birth to a child with a disability, it is a natural reaction to ask "*Why?*" People seek order in their lives and like to think they have some degree of control over what happens. When disability occurs, their understanding of the world is challenged and they look for answers. Lacking medical or scientific answers, people often devise superstitious or mythological explanations, sometimes drawn from religious or cultural traditions: broken taboos, failure to properly revere one's ancestors, witchcraft or the work of evil spirits, sin on the part of the individual or the parents, or God's punishment for sin. Some have even suggested that the child with a severe disability is actually an animal in human form, or was fathered by an animal.[2]

Especially in developing nations, such inaccurate views lead to the person's being victimized by neglect, superstition, inaccurate stereotyping, and/or exploitation. Prejudicial attitudes derived from these cultural beliefs result in the individual, and sometimes the whole family, being ostracized. The outcome may be abandonment or infanticide. When these misconceptions shape the community's thinking, there is a tendency to blame the disabled, seeing the individual (and often the parents) as personally responsible for the condition. Stigma then attaches both to the individual and the family causing them to feel shame or guilt. At the same time, this negative view of disability elevates temporarily able-bodied persons, at least in their own mind, allowing them to justify their rejection or neglect of those affected by disability. Consequently, the person with

---

[2]   One form of cerebral palsy (athetoid) is characterized by slow, writhing, involuntary muscle movement. Typically affecting the hands, feet, arms, or legs, these movements may also affect the tongue and muscles of the face, causing contorted facial expression and drooling. The person may appear restless, as if in constant motion, unable to hold a steady posture. I know of children in Africa with these characteristics whose family believes the child was fathered by a snake or *is* a snake in the guise of a child, and who have emotionally, if not physically, abandoned the child.

the disability is pushed to the margins of society, often even by the Church—exactly opposite to the manner in which Jesus interacted with, even welcomed, persons with disability during his earthly ministry. Hence, individuals with disabilities often find themselves in the same situation as the man in John 5—they have "no one to help them."

The actual causes and correlates of disability are many; some can be identified, but in many cases a specific causal factor is unknown. Typical causes can be grouped into these categories:

- Accidents (e.g., auto accidents, sports injuries, falls)

- Illness (e.g., polio, meningitis, encephalitis, untreated childhood diseases) and lack of immunization against common but preventable diseases

- Genetic abnormalities or problems arising during pregnancy

- Birth complications or injuries during the birth process

- Crime and violent conflict

- Ageing

A multitude of more specific causal elements could be listed under each category, but that lies beyond the scope of this book. Any combination of these factors increases the potential for a disabling condition to result. Each of the conditions listed is further complicated by poverty and malnutrition and/or inadequate or inaccessible health care and social services.

The categories given above suggest possible direct causes of disability. We must remember, however, that these things do not happen apart from the sovereignty of God. They are not totally random happenings occurring without God's knowledge and ultimate control. This will be discussed more in the chapter four where several biblical themes that inform disability ministry are presented.

Categories of Impairment

Medically speaking, impairment or disability encompasses a wide variety of physical, sensory, psychological, and/or intellectual conditions. Different impairments produce different types of functional limitations. People with the same disability may differ significantly in the extent of their impairment, ranging from *mild*, to *moderate*, to *severe or profound*. An individual's culture and environment often affects the specific meaning of these qualifying terms; what is a mild disability in the United States may be more severely limiting in less developed nations.

Disabilities may be *static* (unchanging) or *progressive* (worsening over time). Some disabilities are congenital (from birth) whereas others are acquired (usually through accident or illness). Space does not allow for a detailed exploration of the various disabling conditions.[3] The basic categories of impairments are as follows:

- ***Mobility and health impairments*** are physical and serious health impairments which interfere with many aspects of daily life. Examples include neurological disorders, such

---

[3] For more specific identification of various disabilities, see Hardman, Drew, & Egan (2011), or Kirk, Gallagher, Coleman, & Anastasiow (2012).

as cerebral palsy, seizure disorder, polio, or spinal cord injury; and muscular-skeletal disorders, such as muscular dystrophy, severe arthritis, or amputation.

- *Sensory impairments* include visual (sight) or auditory (hearing) impairments resulting in total or partial loss of function.

- *Cognitive impairments* include mental disabilities such as Down Syndrome; specific learning disabilities, such as dyslexia, wherein a neurological dysfunction affects the ability to process information; and autism, a neurologically-based disorder affecting communication and behavior.

- *Speech and language (communication) impairments* are problems involving articulation of sounds, fluency of speech, or voice quality. These problems also may accompany any of the other impairments, or may be the result of brain injury or stroke.

- *Psychological impairments* include emotional or behavioral disorders resulting from biological/neurological problems or internal (psychological) conflict having an environmental cause, such as child abuse or trauma.

It must be recognized that some individuals may be multiply impaired, meaning they are affected in more than one of the above areas, such as deaf-blind or physically and speech impaired. In ministering to persons and families affected by disability it is helpful to gain some understanding of the specific impairment and how it impacts the individual in his or her environment. The impact on families will be discussed in chapter six.

Going Deeper

1. Read John 5:1–9. Put yourself in the position of the man lying on his mat near the Pool of Bethesda each day hoping to be the first into the pool if an angel stirred the waters. What would your day be like? Is there anyone *you* could count on to help you get into the pool?

    a. Why did Jesus, knowing the man had been there for a long time, *ask* if he wanted to be made well (cured)?

    b. Jesus told the man, "Get up, take up your bed, and walk." Having been disabled for 38 years, we might expect that the man would simply laugh in response to Jesus's command. Possibly, the man had never stood or walked before. But John wrote that immediately (*eutheos*) the man was cured, stood up and walked. What do you think happened to make the man respond without hesitation? Was it simply the Holy Spirit empowering him? Could he feel strengthening in his body?

2. What strengths and weakness are part of your "design"? How are you different from others (family members, co-workers, spouse)? In what type of situation do you feel inadequate or disadvantaged?

3. Do you agree or disagree with the notion that a faulty understanding of 'normalcy' lies at the root of how persons with disabilities are perceived by others? Why or why not?

4. What is your response to the idea that you are *temporarily* able-bodied?

Chapter Two

Human Barriers versus God's View

In the last chapter I explored misconceptions of "normal" and "disabled" and how these color the way people with disabilities are often viewed. The gospels make it clear that Jesus's message was one of acceptance and compassionate love for all people. The gospel writers show Jesus intentionally breaking down gender, racial, and ethnic barriers erected by society and verbally chastising the religious leaders for their lack of concern and oppressive attitudes toward those in need. We see Jesus destroying barriers which separated disabled and able-bodied persons by accepting, caring about them, and curing many. Through his actions and his teaching Jesus "fashioned a new understanding of humanity rooted in the grace of God" (Nolan, 1976, p. 167).

This chapter will uncover several barriers that separate people who are disabled from the community of faith. Attention will then turn to understanding how God views persons who are disabled.

Barriers faced by Persons with a Disability

General barriers faced by individuals and families affected by disability fall into several categories. Some of the more significant barriers of concern to disability ministry are architectural and communication, attitudinal, theological, and inspirational.

Architectural and communication barriers are those which affect the individual's ability to access services or programs within the community or to enter buildings (including churches). Persons with disabilities often lack the opportunity to hear or access God's Word and to attend church because of their disabling condition. In some cases physical access may be difficult or impossible, as with a mobility impairment. Sometimes communication may be the problem, as with deafness or limited vision. Inadequate lighting or inappropriate seating arrangements (because of the building's construction or an uninformed usher seating a person with a disability "out of the way") also fit into this category. Any barrier which affects the person's ability to hear the gospel or to participate in the faith community needs to be addressed and removed.

Attitudinal barriers are those which persons who are temporarily able-bodied erect between themselves and disabled persons. It is not the presence or absence of disability that separates people from one another (nor racial, ethnic, political, cultural, linguistic differences). Rather, the barriers that separate originate within persons who judge themselves to be superior to others in some way. Temporarily able-bodied persons may unfavorably judge those who are disabled because of their misinformed perception of disability and the absence of any relationship with someone who is disabled. Often, this judgment leads to a response of fear, embarrassment, guilt, anger, prejudice, or insensitivity. Disability, although in itself having no moral element, may be viewed as "bad," something negative or evil to be avoided. This easily transfers to the person who is disabled so that the *person* is seen as negative or evil—incomplete, unworthy of life, someone to be ignored or discarded. This attitude displays not only in actions toward persons who are disabled, but also in words used to describe them, which are often based on stereotypes and an assumption that people with disabilities are all alike, all cursed, or any of the other unfavorable ways by which people "interpret" disability. These negative valuations allow temporarily able-bodied persons to make judgments based on their assumption that disabled persons will experience a poor or limited quality of life and to conclude, for example, that to abort a child who may be disabled is being "kind" to the unborn child. In reality, the decision to abort may rest more on how they assume having a disabled child will affect *their own* quality of life. Attitudinal barriers also include the scarcity syndrome discussed in chapter one.

Another type of attitudinal barrier often arises as a result of people's unfamiliarity with disability—or with a particular person who has a disability. This barrier has more to do with ourselves and our fear of interacting with the person because of not knowing what actions are appropriate or needed, especially when the person's disability is severe. The problem does not stem from an attitude of superiority, but from fear that we may do something wrong or unintentionally harmful and concern that we not appear ignorant. While there could be an element of pride in this fear, in one sense it is a more "honest" fear. It is what we *do* with that fear that is important, and either provides an answer or reveals a deeper problem. Asking the individual or his or her attendant or family member how we can be of assistance, how we can serve them, is an appropriate response and communicates respect for the individual. *Not* asking reveals an unwillingness on our part and communicates rejection.

I recall an incident in my own life that occurred many years ago when I spent the summer working in an early intervention program at a rehabilitation hospital. One of the children served was a very young boy who had cerebral palsy that resulted in quadriplegia, the inability to use or control his arms and legs. He would arrive at the program in a stroller that kept his body flexed and in proper position. But removing him from the stroller to a mat where we could provide therapeutic and educational intervention was problematic. My attempt to move him to the mat caused a spastic reaction in the muscles of his entire body: his arms, legs, neck and torso became immediately rigid and hyper-extended. He could not control this reaction or "break" the rigidity of his body, which was unbending. This was obviously uncomfortable for him, and prevented any meaningful intervention. I was fearful that attempting to bend his arms, legs, or hips would "break" him, and did not know how to alter his posture. I had two options: to leave him in that hyper-extended position, or to admit my ignorance and ask for assistance from the physical therapist. I chose the latter and, after she stopped laughing at me in my predicament, she informed me that all that was necessary was a gentle tap behind his knees and in the crook of his arm, and to apply a slight pressure on his abdomen, just above the hips. This caused his muscles to immediately relax into a flexed position, allowing him to participate in the planned activities. And my embarrassment at not knowing how to help quickly subsided.

Closely related to attitudinal barriers are **theological barriers**. These come as a result of the lack of accurate information about actual causes of disability and from not having a proper biblical understanding of disability. Few Christians have persons with disabilities included in their circle of friends, and few Christians, not faced directly with disability, spend time looking at Scripture from a disability perspective.[4] Sometimes this is due to difficulty reconciling belief in a sovereign, loving, all-powerful God and the presence of disability; other times it is based on an incorrect understanding or misapplication of Scriptural teaching, perhaps even misinterpreting verses by taking them out of context. The assumption that personal sin and disability or suffering are always directly linked is another aspect of theological barriers. Such incorrect theological and attitudinal beliefs prevent a person who is disabled from being fully integrated into the community of faith. This book is intended to help people develop a biblical and theological understanding of disability allowing them to engage in appropriate ministry to and with individuals and families affected by disability.

Also closely related to attitudinal barriers, are **aspirational barriers** which stem from how individuals who have a disability view themselves, and the impact of that self-assessment on their personal goals, desires, and feelings of self-worth. To a great extent, the individual's self-concept and aspirations are derived from the attitudes of and treatment by others who are not disabled. Many persons who are disabled will not attempt to go to church, or will stop going to church after becoming disabled, because they fear negative reactions of temporarily able-bodied parishioners. Sometimes, they feel *dis-invited* or *unwelcome* at the church because of the reactions or stares of others. Some who become disabled may not believe they are capable of achieving anything of significance and assume they can contribute little or nothing to the Body of Christ. Part of an effective ministry to persons who are disabled will involve challenging these faulty views and encouraging Christians who are or who become disabled to discover ways in which they may fellowship and serve alongside those who are more able-bodied.

If there are any barriers of attitude, communication, or architecture for *anyone*, then the foundations of the House of God is weakened. God said, "My house shall be called a house of prayer for all peoples" (Isaiah 56:7). *All peoples* includes those with disabilities. Recognizing specific barriers in one's heart and in one's church, and determining how these barriers can be removed, gives direction to disability ministry. One way to bring positive change is to understand how God views people with disabilities.

God's View of Persons with Disabilities

Church leaders must model and teach a biblically sound perspective on disability issues. In this section, several basic ideas are introduced regarding how God views individuals who have a disability. Chapters three and four more deeply explore key biblical and theological themes that inform disability ministry.

People with disabilities (and their families) are as equally valued and valuable as those who are temporarily able-bodied: <u>All</u> people are created in the image of God. As was said earlier, there are only two kinds of people, those who are disabled and those who are temporarily

---

[4]   An excellent example of looking at the Bible through the lens of disability is Yong (2011).

able-bodied. Despite the severity of a disability, the two groups are more alike than different. One commonality is that both are created in the image of God, giving them intrinsic worth. The value of human beings lies not in a person's abilities, fortune, achievement, family heritage and status, or any other humanly prized attribute. Our value comes solely from God's having created us in his image. The Bible does not suggest that someone born with a disability is less than human, nor does it teach that the image of God is relative to some standard of normalcy. God's image in human beings is neither diminished by disability nor confirmed by ability. The most intelligent person is no more God's image than the most severely cognitively impaired person. "The Christian understanding of human beings as created in the image of God bestows dignity and honor on every person, regardless of social, mental, or physical status" (Shelley & Miller, 1999, pp. 61–62).

Closely aligned with being created in the image of God is the idea that **God does not measure persons by what they <u>do</u>, <u>can do</u>, or <u>cannot do</u>**. We can do nothing that will make God love us any *more* or any *less* than he does at this moment. God's love is perfect and unconditional. It does not depend on what we do or fail to do. Educator and theologian Henri Nouwen asserted that each of us is unique, known and loved by the One who fashioned us (Nouwen, 1997). God does not want us as his children because of our strength or ability or intelligence (all of which are from God in the first place). God simply wants our love, our fellowship, our worship—things which all can give him, regardless of able-bodiedness or disability. Limitations or disabilities do not define us; in a sense they are irrelevant. Whether disabled or temporarily able-bodied, as believers, we belong to God purely by his grace (cf. Ephesians 2:8–10). What is important is what God intends to do through us, even through our weakness.

God values our weakness because it is through our weakness that his power can be displayed. God's revealed truth is frequently paradoxical—it does not match the way the world thinks. For example, Jesus said "many who are first will be last, and the last first" (Matthew 19:30) and "let the greatest among you become as the youngest, and the leader as one who serves" (Luke 22:26). Paul said "God chose what is weak in the world to shame the strong" (1 Corinthians 2:7), using the word *astheneia* which, as we have already noted, includes the idea of feebleness or disability. In 2 Corinthians 12, Paul related his struggle with a disabling condition and how he sought God's removal of his "thorn in the flesh." God's answer was "No," but he then gave Paul insight into another paradox: God explained that his power is made perfect or complete in Paul's weakness—or as one translation puts it, "When you are weak, my power is made perfect in you" (2 Corinthians 12:9, NCV). It is in our weakness, our limitations, that we most clearly experience God's strength. God is a jealous God and will not share his glory with anyone or anything (Exodus 34:14; Deuteronomy 4:24). Any "power" we have in ourselves comes to an end so that God alone receives honor by acting through us. Moving forward relying on our own self-effort, as if blinded by our own strength, can hinder God's activity. When God looks upon someone who is disabled, he does not see them as having limited value or possibility; he sees someone through whom he can display his greatness.

Because of his great love and because he can demonstrate his power and glory through human weakness, **God desires that people with disabilities serve in his kingdom**. Paul drew an analogy between the human body and the Church of Christ in 1 Corinthians 12:12–26 in which he underscored the importance of the "weaker" members to the functioning of the whole body. Members of the church body who are disabled could be included in the *weaker members*. Temporarily able-bodied members of the Body of Christ may feel that those who are weaker (disabled) are unimportant, unnecessary, or unneeded. Even believers who are disabled may feel less honorable or presentable, less able to serve God. But these are the very ones on whom God bestows greater honor and who, in God's view, are necessary for his kingdom. It is essential that believers have a biblically informed perspective on disability so that negative attitudes toward people who are disabled do not result in devaluing these essential members of the Body of Christ. Just as God designed each human body with intention (cf. Psalm 139:13–15), so he has constructed and pieced together the Body of Christ with intention: "God arranged the members in the body, each one of them, as he chose" (1 Corinthians 12:18).

God's compassion for persons who are disabled or otherwise oppressed is clearly shown throughout Scripture (cf. Psalm 9:9, 103:6; Isaiah 1:17). **God's desire is that we display the same compassion to persons with disabilities as Jesus did.** Jesus seemed almost to go out of his way to interact with individuals who were diseased, disabled, or otherwise pushed aside by society. His approaching the man by the Pool of Bethesda (John 5) is but one instance. The Gospels are replete with other examples of Jesus taking time to minister to persons marginalized by the leaders of the Jews. A cursory review of the Gospel of Mark reveals that nearly 17% of the verses show Jesus interacting with disabled or diseased persons or teaching on related issues. Of the 35 recorded miracles of Jesus in the New Testament, 23 involved persons with a disability. This gives strong indications of God's heart for people whose lives are affected by disability.

We conclude from this that **the Gospel is fully inclusive; it is a message of life and hope for all people.** Christ demonstrated the highest form of inclusiveness, breaking down barriers of gender, race, ethnicity, and ability/disability—reaching those the world might see as "the least." Jesus's direct teaching in Luke 14:12–14, further illustrated in the parable of the great banquet (Luke 14:16–24), shows that Jesus desires that his Church reach people with disabilities, not just able-bodied persons. John 3:16 gives an inclusive answer to the question "Who does God love and who can receive eternal life?" Jesus's commission of his disciples (then and now) to preach the Gospel to the whole world excludes no one from its scope. Church leaders must not restrict their evangelistic, church-building interests solely to persons who, in their judgment, are best able to "feed" the church (financially or otherwise). The Great Commission is clear: the gospel message is to be taken to every people group (Matthew 28:18, Mark 16:15). To be faithful to our Lord and obedient to his command we must seek to cross barriers and break down walls of separation. The gospel, in all its fullness, must be shared with individuals who are disabled as readily as it is shared with those who are temporarily able-bodied. Jesus said to his disciples, "I came that they may have life and have it abundantly" (John 10:10b). Here, Jesus is speaking of something much larger and more important than having a life free of disability, pain, or suffering. The fullness of life which Jesus gives goes beyond our circumstances and is not limited by disability.

It is important to remember that **the gospel in its fullness includes seeking justice for those who are oppressed by society, by culture, and by Satan.** It is not simply a call to receive Christ as Lord and Savior. God's concern for social justice is found throughout the Scriptures. John Perkins (1976) pointed to two themes that thread their way though the Bible: God's concern for truth, seen in his hatred of idolatry, and God's concern for the poor and oppressed. Both themes are relevant to our understanding of how God views people who are disabled and what our response to them must be. Many temporarily able-bodied have an idealized (even *idolized*) view of the "whole" body, and most people like to believe that they have some degree of control over their body and their circumstances. Meeting a person with a visible disability is a reminder that this control is more fictitious than real. We are all vulnerable to accidents, illnesses, genetic weaknesses and predispositions which can result in a disabling condition, and we all grow older. To preserve their psychological comfort and maintain their idolized view of self and body, many turn their back to those who have a disability, overtly or covertly pushing them away, in an effort to sustain their own comfort level. We must remember Micah's words, "what does the LORD require of you but to do justice, and to love kindness, and to walk humbly with your God?" (Micah 6:8).

God's vision for the disabled is not limited to this world. Isaiah 35:3–6 presents a picture of the restoration and redemption of Israel that was symbolically fulfilled when God brought the Jewish people back from captivity. The complete fulfillment will come when the Kingdom of Christ is fully established. Some have understood Isaiah to be speaking of spiritual blindness and deafness only. But the ministry of Jesus marked the beginning of the fulfillment of the promise as some who were actually blind received their sight, some who were deaf and mute were enabled to hear and speak, and others were restored to physical strength, such as the man in John 5. Jesus said that the Kingdom was "near" (Mark 1:15; Luke 10:9, 11) or "within" (Luke 17:21). The Kingdom was present because King Jesus was present, and believers have become a part of that kingdom. But its growth will not be complete until Jesus returns to consummate God's plan. Isaiah 35:3–6 and similar passages picture that new age of which only the redeemed will partake. They promise the removal of disability when Christ's Kingdom is complete and all is restored to its perfect, pre-Genesis 3 state. We must be cautious not to press this point too strongly, however. While it can and should bring hope to someone who is disabled, there is a danger that they may conclude that they are not acceptable (to us, to themselves, or to God) in their present disabled body, that they are not as "good" as temporarily able-bodied believers, or that they have nothing to offer to the community of faith. Many Christians are familiar with the hymn "Just as I am, without one plea but that thy blood was shed for me." Few are aware, however, that this well-know hymn was written by Charlotte Elliot, a woman in poor health and frequent pain. Despite having had a severe illness that left her permanently disabled, she knew she was loved and accepted by God *just as she was,* and the words of her song have contributed to the spiritual journey of many. Tony Evans aptly commented:

> In God's economy, all is redeemed and nothing is ever lost. He can take the good things that we remember most fondly, the bad things we might like to forget, and the ugly things that have shaped us into people we didn't start out to be and use *all of them* to facilitate His individual purpose for each and every one of us. (Evans, 2002, p. 12, emphasis in the original).

Going Deeper

Questions about barriers:

1. What *architectural* or *communication* barriers are there at your church which would prevent people with disabilities from sharing in worship? Begin to explore ways by which those barriers can be eliminated. What must be done to allow and to encourage people with disabilities to become a part of your faith community?

2. What *attitudinal* or *theological* barriers exist in your own heart and mind? What prejudices do you need to repent of?

3. If you are a church leader, how can you bring change in the minds and hearts of your congregation so that they are open to welcoming persons with disabilities into their fellowship.

For Discussion:

1. Leviticus 19:14 says, "You shall not curse the deaf or put a stumbling block before the blind, but you shall fear your God: I am the LORD." Is this an admonition to remove barriers to full inclusion and participation of persons with disabilities in the Christian Church and in worship?

2. Proverbs 22:6 says, "Train up a child in the way he should go; even when he is old he will not depart from it." This implies modifying the curriculum and teaching methods or adapting the presentation of the gospel to accommodate individual needs and differences. It could be considered a mandate to provide "special education" in the church for those who are disabled. The reference to a "child" does not imply that people with disabilities are childlike. The principle easily applies to spiritual "children" (new believers), regardless of age.

3. Romans 10:14 says "How then will they call on him in whom they have not believed? And how are they to believe in him of whom they have never heard? And how are they to hear without someone preaching?" The command to preach the gospel to all peoples includes sharing with people who have severe hearing impairments. How are we to understand Paul's words *preach* and *hear*? Is Paul of the opinion that a person who cannot hear cannot receive the gospel? How can the message of the gospel be presented ("preached") so that someone who is totally deaf can understand and receive ("hear") the message and express belief in Christ?

4. In Luke 19:45–46 we read of Jesus driving from the temple those who were selling, saying "It is written, 'My house shall be a house of prayer,' but you have made it a den of robbers" (quoting from Jeremiah 7:11). If our theological misunderstandings about disability and our attitude toward people who are disabled result in not welcoming or in preventing such persons from participating in our community of faith, have we become a "den of thieves,"

robbing them of the opportunity to hear the gospel message and fellowship with other believers?

5. Take time to explore the Gospel records and note the many times Jesus is shown interacting with someone with a disability or a disease—persons who, because of their condition were cut off from the mainstream of society. How does your attitude toward people with disabilities compare with that of Jesus?

Section Two

Biblical Themes to Inform Disability Ministry

Chapter Three

The Nature and Character of God and Humankind

From now on, therefore, we regard no one according to the flesh. Even though we once regarded Christ according to the flesh, we regard him thus no longer. Therefore, if anyone is in Christ, he is a new creation. The old has passed away; behold, the new has come. All this is from God, who through Christ reconciled us to himself and gave us the ministry of reconciliation; that is, in Christ God was reconciling the world to himself, not counting their trespasses against them, and entrusting to us the message of reconciliation. (2 Corinthians 5:16–17)

Biblical teaching on living and loving, on relationships with God and fellow humans, and on sin, grace, and forgiveness all have direct relevance to the Christian life and the ministry of reconciliation to which we have been called. When Paul wrote "we regard no one according to the flesh," it is unlikely that he was thinking about disability. But as I have stressed in the last two chapters, many who are temporarily able-bodied view people who are disabled negatively. If we are truly interested in ministering to and with people with disabilities, we must see them through God's eyes, not "fleshly" eyes. Hence, I see this passage from 2 Corinthians as especially relevant to disability ministry. An inclusive biblical worldview focuses on reconciliation of people to God, as well as reconciliation between individuals—in our focus, between disabled and non disabled persons. We recognize that persons with disabilities *and* persons who are temporarily able-bodied are equally in need of the God's grace.

This chapter and the next explore familiar biblical and theological themes. Rather than an exhaustive study of doctrinal teaching, however, they are presented as beginning points for your theological reflection of disability and disability ministry. My intent is to help you see biblical and theological teaching with disability in mind. I hope to challenge your assumptions and to help you gain an understanding of disability from God's perspective. This will help you to recognize that churches and individuals must minister to *all* people. We begin by considering the sovereignty and character of God, then move on to examine biblical teaching about humankind. Chapter four will focus on biblical principles especially relevant to disability ministry, and explore general themes that place disability ministry squarely within the realm of Christian activity. Interspersed among the discussion are questions for your reflection designed to help you see implications of biblical thought to disability.

Theme: The Nature and Character of God

A. The Sovereignty of God

A Christian worldview acknowledges God as Creator of all that is, and God as the Sovereign Ruler of the universe (cf. Genesis 1:1–2:25; Psalm 103:19; Isaiah 40:28; Colossians 1:16). The very first words of the Bible—Genesis 1:1, "In the beginning God"—capture in seed form the greatness and sovereignty of God. Paul states in Romans 11:36 that all things are "from him and through him and to him," indicating that all is intended to bring God glory and honor. Through his sovereign power, God created and actively sustains the world, directing events toward the fulfillment of his master-plan: to bring all things under the authority of Jesus Christ (Ephesians 1:10). Thus, God is intimately involved in the lives of his people (cf. Colossians 1:17).

It is the clear teaching of scripture that God is involved in the creation of every child, that God "made everything beautiful in its time" (Ecclesiastes 3:11), and that "children are a heritage [gift] from the LORD" (Psalm 127:3). The words of David masterfully depict God's involvement in the creation of each individual:

> For you formed my inward parts; you knitted me together in my mother's womb. I praise you, for I am fearfully and wonderfully made. Wonderful are your works; my soul knows it very well. My frame was not hidden from you, when I was being made in secret, intricately woven in the depths of the earth. Your eyes saw my unformed substance; in your book were written, every one of them, the days that were formed for me, when as yet there was none of them. (Psalm 139:13–16)

To say that we are "fearfully" and "wonderfully" made captures the awesomeness and distinctiveness of humankind as the highest of God's created beings. David described each person as individually embroidered by God, which implies obvious intent in God's weaving each person in the womb. Our "frame" (Psalm 139:15) has reference not just to our skeletal structure or physicality, but also to our intellect, emotions, talents, and abilities. Each person is individually pieced together according to God's design (intent). David said that our "days" were written in God's book, indicating not simply the length of our lives but the tasks which God has planned for our undertaking (cf. Ephesians 2:10; Philippians 2:12–13), plans which come from God's loving heart and have our best interest and his own glory in mind (Wiersbe, 2004, Psalm 139).

But suppose a woman gives birth to a child who has a severe mental or physical impairment. Or suppose a person becomes disabled as the result of an injury, illness, or violence. Do these events challenge scripture's view of God as sovereign and loving? How can scenarios such as these be reconciled with the idea that God is completely sovereign? Is a child born with a disabling condition an exception to the rule? Did God make a mistake or lose control? Did God cause that disability-causing injury? If he did not cause it, why did he allow it to happen? Questions such as these, and the uncertainty they reflect, are understandable reactions when faced with a disability, especially given people's natural desire to understand their experiences and maintain some sense of order in their lives. The questions are not important only to people directly involved with disability. Non disabled believers must also consider such questions in order to counsel, encourage, or comfort those affected by disability—and because everyone is vulnerable to injury or illness-induced disability.

In dealing with these issues, it is important to maintain our belief that God is infinite, eternal, and unchangeable in all his attributes even when a child is born with a disability or when someone becomes disabled through illness or injury. Disabling conditions are often the natural consequence of living in a sinful, fallen world (see the discussion of the problem of evil and suffering in chapter eight). But David's words in Psalm 139 also allow that congenital impairments are a part of God's design. Combine David's thought with God's response when Moses sought to evade God's commission to seek Pharaoh's release of the Jews from captivity. Moses appealed to his speech difficulty as an excuse from doing what God asked. But God replied, "Who has made man's mouth? Who makes him mute, or deaf, or seeing, or blind? Is it not I, the LORD?" (Exodus 4:11). This passage makes it clear that God, for reasons know only to him, is ultimately beneath congenital disability. It also is a declaration that God honors persons who have disabilities; from God's perspective, disability is not a tragedy. The point is that God "makes all people, regardless of abilities or disabilities. He loves them equally and claims them equally as His special creation" (Palau, 1999, pp. 42–43). God, having individually designed each person, sees beauty and worth in *every* individual, as well as their potential for bringing glory to himself, regardless of ability or disability. Disability, even from birth, is not outside God's sovereignty or foreknowledge, nor does it preclude a person affected by disability from living a meaningful life. God does not make mistakes!

God's sovereignty is not in question because of disability. We have no reason to assume that God was "absent" when a child is born with a handicapping condition. Exactly *how* God is involved in the creation of each child we are not told, nor are we told *why* God does not intervene in the embryonic or fetal development to correct or overrule a genetic defect or prenatal insult. However, any notion that God has made a mistake, which would bring his sovereignty and wisdom into question, must be dismissed.

Also to be rejected is the thought that God punishes people for sin by disabling their child. This is to accuse God of acting arbitrarily rather than righteously and implies that a "whole" or non disabled person is of greater value or worth to God. Many people hold to an incorrect understanding of Scripture, believing that in this life, God will bless those who are righteous with prosperity and health, but will punish those who are sinners. They conclude, therefore, that disability is a sign that either the person or the parents are being judged for sin. This was the argument of Job's counselors, that he suffered because of unconfessed sin, and of the disciples who asked Jesus if the man was born blind because of his own sin or that of his parents (John 9:1–2). Such assumptions are challenged by the Bible's declaration that "all have sinned and fall short of the glory of God" (Romans 3:23) and that no one can claim to be righteous based on their own merit (Isaiah 64:6–7; Romans 1:18–2:1). To assert that disability is causally connected to sin would raise the question why *everyone* is not disabled. It is essential to remember that it was while we were "dead in our trespasses" that God, in grace, mercy, and love, saved us (Ephesians 2:4–10)—not because we were spiritually alive and deserving of God's grace.

> ### *For Further Reflection:*
>
> - Read Psalm 104 in connection with the account of creation in Genesis 1–2. Meditate on what the psalmist declares about God's creative activity and sovereign care for his creation. In his classic devotional, *Waiting for God,* Andrew Murray (1895, Day 3) wrote, "The one object for which God gave life to creatures was that in them he might prove and show forth his wisdom, power, and goodness." Consider how God can show his wisdom, power, and goodness to and even *through* persons who are disabled.
>
> - What does Paul assert in Romans 8:28 about God's ability to bring good out of any situation? How does this apply to our understanding of how disability and God's sovereignty relate?
>
> - What was Jesus's response in John 9:1–3 when asked by his disciples whether the man was born blind because of his own sin or sin of his parents? How does this affect your view of disability?

B. The Goodness of God

God is also revealed in the Bible to be infinite, eternal, holy, omniscient, omnipotent, omnipresent, and immutable (unchanging). God is infinite, eternal, and unchangeable in all his attributes. Goodness is an essential quality of God's character. His sovereignty, wisdom, love, grace, and goodness are not threatened when a child is born with a disability or a person acquires a disability through accident, disease, or ageing. Nor is God's essential goodness challenged if he does not miraculously intervene to prevent or correct a disabling condition.

One of my former colleagues was informed that her unborn child had Down Syndrome, a genetic condition which can result in physical problems, developmental delay, and cognitive impairment. This news shook, but did not weaken, her faith—just as Job's theology was challenged, but his belief in God remained. She questioned whether it was appropriate for her to ask God to reconstruct the chromosomal structure of each cell in her unborn child, or simply to trust God and ask that he give her a heart of love for the child. As she wrestled with this situation, she grew in her assurance of God's ongoing love, goodness, and presence despite what lie ahead. (Her son does indeed have Down Syndrome. It would deny reality to say he does not present her with challenges at times, but he is a loving boy and a welcomed part of her family.)

Applied to God, *goodness* describes how he freely relates to us through the covenant of grace and promises to remain loving, just, merciful, faithful, and forgiving. We rejoice in the goodness of God (2 Chronicles 6:41), for his goodness endures forever (2 Chronicles 7:3). God's goodness to all people includes his *common grace* whereby he "makes his sun rise on the evil and on the good, and sends rain on the just and on the unjust" (Matthew 5:45). And God's goodness is shown in his special (saving) grace on believers (Ephesians 2:8–10). John Piper (2012) linked God's sovereignty and his goodness, saying:

> Since God is sovereign and has promised *not to turn away from doing good to his covenant people*, we can know beyond all doubt, in tribulation and distress and persecution and famine and nakedness and peril and sword [and, for our purposes we can add "disability"], that we are more than conquerors through him who loved us (Romans 8:35–37). (p. 172, emphasis in the original)

God is good despite what occurs in our lives. Like God, however, his goodness is something which created beings cannot fully grasp (cf. Isaiah 55:8–9). God's goodness differs from our subjective feeling of "happiness" or what we consider "kindness." Jesus taught in his sermon on the mount (Matthew 5) that true happiness is found in relation to and in submission to the Lord, not in the possession of things or in living a life of ease. When we understand the faithfulness of God we proclaim with David, "Surely goodness and mercy shall follow me all the days of my life, and I shall dwell in the house of the LORD forever" (Psalm 23:6). God has not promised to be as good or charitable as possible to as many as possible, nor to prevent or remove all suffering or pain, but he has promised that he will never leave or forsake his people (Joshua 1:5; Hebrews 13:5). Rather than happiness Paul stressed contentment (cf. Philippians 4:11–12). Knowing that God is with us even in the midst of life's struggles or disabling conditions brings encouragement and hope to those who face affliction or uncertainty. The Bible gives strong assurance, through precept and example, that God's sovereignty, wisdom, love, and grace are not threatened by disability, nor is his goodness challenged if he does not intervene to prevent or to cure a disabling condition.

For Further Reflection:

- Consider what these verses reveal about the goodness of the Lord: Psalm 25:8; 34:8; 54:6; 86:5; 100:5; 106:1; 107:1; 118:1, 29; 119:68; 135:3; 136:1; 143:10; 145:9

- If God is good, as these verses suggest, what should be our response if we, or a member of our family, become disabled—of if we have a child who is born with a disability?

Theme: Nature and Character of Humankind

A. The Intrinsic Worth: The Image of God

The Bible teaches that we are made in the image of God (Genesis 1:26–28, 31; 2:7). God has created *each* person as a reflection of himself. We mirror God; that is, we are meant to represent God, to make him "visible" on earth. When humankind is what we were designed to be, people should be able to see something of God's love, kindness, and goodness. Humankind was to represent God by expressing the authority of God; advancing God's program for the world; supporting and defending what God stands for; and promoting what God desires (Hoekema, 1986).

Scholars have proposed four views of what it means to be in the image of God, though they are not mutually exclusive. The more traditional understanding of the image of God is the **substantive view**, which focuses on characteristics of humankind that mirror in limited fashion characteristics of God. These "communicable" attributes include such things as the ability to reason, communication, imagination, and creativity.

Closely associated with the substantive view is the **functional view** of the image of God, which stresses dominion and stewardship. Adam was assigned the role of manager or steward over all that God had created (Genesis 1:28, 2:15). God charged Adam (humankind) with the responsibility of caring for and cultivating creation—exploring, discovering, and using wisely all the possibilities that God "hid" within his creation. This provided the opportunity and responsibility to use our abilities (our "design," as we saw in Psalm 139:13–16) in cooperation with God through faithful stewardship (Wiersbe, 2001c).

A third perspective on the image of God is the **relational view,** which emphasizes relationship with God and others. The essential nature of relationship is love: we were created to love God and show that love in our interaction with others (Mark 12:29–31). This also entails spiritual elements by which Christians are to image the Father: mercy (Luke 6:36), love (1 John 4:8–11), holiness (1 Peter 1:15–16), and service (John 13:14–17).

The **teleological view** of the image of God accentuates the end or purpose for human existence. Essentially, that end or goal is to bring glory to God (cf. Nehemiah 9:5–6; Psalm 148). Piper (2003) explained that God created humankind "to live our lives in a way that makes him look more like the greatness and the beauty that he really is . . . . We are meant to image forth in the world what he is really like" (pp. 32–33). The image of God in humankind is a present reality, though the image is tarnished by the Fall (Genesis 3). This view acknowledges that Christ fully embodied that image (John 1:14, 14:9; 2 Corinthians 4:4; Colossians 1:15; Hebrews 1:3), and that believers are now being conformed to be like Christ.

A summary of the meaning of the image of God is given by Estep (2010):

God's image within humanity is what we *are* and, in turn, is reflected in the components of our existence, relational capacity with one another and God, in our function to fulfill God's expressed purpose for humanity, and even in the eschatological reality that awaits us. (p. 19, emphasis in original)

Our worth as human beings lies in the fact we are God's image, which confers dignity and honor on all, without regard to our social, mental, or physical condition. *All* persons have value before God—not as an earned status based on ability, intelligence, appearance, or other humanly-valued characteristic, but simply because we bear the image of God. People's fallen (sinful) human nature leads them to establish hierarchies to rank people. People tend to elevate themselves above others—which means that others are consciously viewed as inferior to them. But God does not recognize such distinctions: All people are equally his by creation, equally in his image, and equally in need of a Savior.

Being God's image refers to who we are in all our fullness: "God didn't create us *in* the image; he created us *as* his image . . . . To be human is to be the image of God, the representative of the Creator" (Clark & Emmett, 1998, p. 115). Our value or worth derives from being part of the human family, where each person—regardless of intellectual capacity, physical mobility, sensory ability, personal attractiveness, or tribal or family lineage—*is* the image of God. There is no circumstance that removes or limits the dignity of human beings and the consequent right to be respected, even for individuals who are disabled because of profound and multiple impairments. "Bearing God's image establishes for every person a fundamental dignity which cannot be undermined by wrongdoing or neediness" (Pohl, 1999, p. 65).

Reynolds (2008) expressed a broad view of what it means to be created in the image of God that is instructive for our consideration of disability:

> [T]o be created in the image of God means to be created for contributing to the world, open toward the call to love others. Three dimensions are implied: creativity with others, relation to others, and availability to others. The point to be stressed is that *all people* can be contributors, representing a range of both gifts and limitations. *Disability is not an incomplete humanity in this regard.* (p. 177, emphasis added)

In sharing his experience of caring for Adam, a young man with severe disabilities, Henri Nouwen encouraged his readers to consider what it means to be created in the image of God—to reflect on the uniqueness of each individual and the true meaning of humanity. He suggested that God reveals himself through and in even the most disabled of persons:

> Adam's humanity was not diminished by his disabilities. Adam's humanity was a full humanity, in which the fullness of love became visible for me . . . . We were friends, brothers, bonded in our hearts. Adam's love was pure and true. It was the same as the love that was mysteriously visible in Jesus, which healed everyone who touched him. (Nouwen, 1997, pp. 50–51)

Because humankind bears the image of God, Christians must have transformed attitudes toward people, characterized by dignity and respect for all of human life, and transformed behaviors, characterized by appreciation for the diversity of people we encounter (Habermas, 1993). Scripture suggests that God highly values those whom we tend to see of lesser importance (cf. Deuteronomy 14:28–29; God's judgment on the nations as recorded in the prophets). Proverbs 14:31 tells us that to oppress the poor is to show contempt for their Maker, but kindness to the needy brings honor to God. That what we do "unto the least of these" is in some way done unto the Lord is emphatic in Jesus's teaching in Matthew 25:34–40. Persons who have a disability logically are included in the groups Jesus mentioned in that parable. Showing love and compassion to these individuals honors God because they, like us, are creatures of worth who bear the image and likeness of their Maker.

For Further Reflection:

- What attitudes do you have which need to be transformed?

- What in your behavior needs to be transformed?

B. The Meaning of Life

Does our life have meaning and purpose? Does having a disability mean the person has no purpose? Scripture teaches that God had a purpose for creating the world. It follows, then, that there must be a God-given meaning or purpose for each human life. People tend to take an anthropocentric (human-centered) position and assume that God created the world for their enjoyment, that God's ultimate purpose is to make us happy by satisfying all our desires. But such a view is not supported by God's Word, which takes a theocentric (God-centered) view and shows God's ultimate purpose is to bring glory to himself.

> We do not exist for ourselves—we exist *for* the Father and *through* the Son. [1 Corinthians 8:6] The world tells us that we derive our existence from it and that we should live for ourselves, but the Word teaches us that all we are and have comes from the Father who formed us for his pleasure and purposes. (Boa, 2001, p. 153, emphasis in original)

What were God's purposes? God created the world in order to display the fullness of his glory, so that people should know, enjoy, and praise God as they come to understand his greatness through exploration of all that he has made. Through humanity's exploration and discovery of all that God has "built into" his creation, and as scientific advances are made, we learn something of the mind of God and are moved to praise him for his imaginative and creative work.

We must acknowledge that God created a world in which disability is possible, though it did not become *actual* until the perfect world God created was altered as a result of Adam and Eve's sinful action (Genesis 3). But this is not necessarily adverse, and it certainly does not reflect faulty design or handiwork on God's part. Having a disability does not prevent a person from affirming God's glory and goodness. We recognize that the world is contingent, limited, and finite and does not exist apart from God's creative will. But these qualities (contingency, limitedness, and finitude) are not necessarily evil, despite the fact that suffering, evil, and disability may result (cf. Yong, 2007). As said earlier, God's power is made manifest in our weakness (2 Corinthians 2:7–10). To glorify God does not require a whole body or even a "whole" mind. God is able to use what the world perceives as weak and insignificant to accomplish great things; the difficulty is that many, viewing the disability and the person in a negative way, do not have "ears to hear" nor "eyes to see."

Our basic human nature leads us to seek coherence and purpose in life—to make things "fit" into an understandable scheme. People who have a disability are often viewed as inferior, leading some to ask what purpose or meaning there could be in the life of someone with a severe disability. Such a question reflects an assumption that being disabled prevents a person from living a meaningful life. But does having a disability limit or prohibit "meaningful existence" (a concept which also needs definition)? This assumption of temporarily able-bodied persons, whether out of ignorance or prejudice, may be more limiting to disabled persons than their impairment. For some, having a disability may actually empower rather than limit. People with disabilities can teach us much about God, grace, compassion, service and sacrifice, even community. We must be careful not to "overlook the wealth of wisdom and experience the disabled have to offer," especially in their testimony to the sufficiency of God's grace (Dignan & Dignan, 2007). Those without disabilities can learn to recognize their own shortcomings and fragility, and our mutual dependence upon God for daily life and breath. Care must be taken not to look at persons with a disability from a position of false superiority or power, but to see them as equals in the sight of God. We also must take care, lest we begin to think of persons with disabilities as "object lessons" and miss seeing their beauty and giftedness. In chapter nine I will explore the idea that being disabled can actually be an *advantage*, rather than a limitation to spiritual growth and faithful living before the Lord.

C. Giftedness and Stewardship

God has uniquely designed every person, giving to each unique abilities, gifts, and talents, as well as limitations and weaknesses. This is true whether the person is able-bodied or has a disability. The Bible refers to God as a potter and humankind as the clay, personally molded according to his design (Isaiah 29:16, 41:25, 45:9, 64:8; Romans 9:21). This image of God carefully handcrafting each individual corresponds to David's assertion in Psalm 139:13–16 that we have been woven in the womb by the hand of God. Both attest to God's personal involvement in the fashioning of each person, showing deliberate intent in our design and attention to every detail.

When God created Adam and Eve (Genesis 1–2), they were given the position of vice-regents or trustees of all that God had created. They were "under-rulers." God was not absenting himself from final control and authority, but appointed Adam and Eve as stewards or managers to administer God's "estate." As agents of and responsible to the Creator, they were expected to demonstrate good stewardship through exploring, developing, and using wisely God's world as servant-managers. This role has not diminished because of the Fall. It has become more difficult, but it has also become more necessary for Christians. We recognize that nothing is "ours"—it all belongs to God. God expects us to exercise principles of good stewardship as we use all that he has given us as individually designed and gifted persons, and all that he has made available to us in the world, so that he will receive honor and glory.

In addition to the innate talents, abilities, and interests which God has designed into each individual, God has also given Spiritual gifts to every believer (1 Corinthians 12:4–11). Scripture does not suggest that the distribution of spiritual gifts was only to persons of sound mind and body. These gifts have been given *for the common good* (1 Corinthians 12:7), which means they are to be used, not buried for safekeeping, as was done by the "wicked and lazy" servant in Jesus's parable (Matthew 25:14–20).

Good stewardship also requires providing assistance or instruction to others in order to enable them to develop to their full potential. The Church must identify and encourage the use of God-given talents and spiritual gifts in all persons, including those whom the world wrongly sees as having lesser value or as objects of pity. Consider this simple illustration of God using someone with a disability in the church:

> Dorothy was a perpetual member of the third grade church school class. Every child in the church knew that, when you arrived at the third grade in the primary division of the . . . Sunday School, Dorothy would be in your class. She had even been in the class when some of our parents were in the third grade. Dorothy was in charge of handing out pencils, checking names in the roll book, and taking up the pencils. We thought she was the teacher's assistant. It was much later, when we were nearly all grown up and adult, that the world told us that Dorothy was someone with Down Syndrome . . . When Dorothy died, in her early fifties . . . the whole church turned out for her funeral. No one mentioned that Dorothy was retarded or afflicted. Many testified to how fortunate they had been to know her. (Hauerwas & Willimon, 1989, p. 93)

Dorothy may not have been great in the eyes of the world, but she used what she had to serve the Lord and, as suggested in the quote, touched the lives of many.

God created man in a state of innocence, declaring his creation of humans "very good" (Gen 1:31). Even if God's fashioning someone in the womb includes a disability, that does not negate the individual's being in the image of God, or suggest that the person has no value. As previously noted, God is good by nature; nothing he does can be construed as being anything but good and in accord with his purpose and decree. Neither ability nor disability alters God's pleasure in what he has created—nor does disability interfere with our ability to find joy in the Lord. Humankind was created for God's pleasure—to celebrate God who is worthy "to receive glory, honor, and power, for [he] created all things, and by [his] will they exist" (Revelation 4:11). Piper commented that humankind is "made for the soul-satisfying glory of God in the gospel" (Piper, 1998, p. 39). For us to glorify God does not require a whole body or "whole" mind; our weakness, in fact, provides a means by which God can bring glory to himself. In reflecting on disability, Browne (1997) raised this provocative thought:

> May not the presence of imperfection be a vibrant indication that something more, something radically transcendent to finite measures, lies just beyond? Can't we see that this apparent design aberration does not deflect God's beauty, God's ineffable perfection, but simply evidences our lack of imagination, our limited finite capabilities? (p. 35)

For Further Reflection:

- Read Matthew 25:14–30 and reflect on the following thoughts, then respond to the questions below. The master "entrusted *his* property" to the servants (just as God has entrusted the world to humankind). The master had a definite expectation that his servants would use and develop (improve) the talents they received. There was diversity in the distribution of the talents. Each servant was given according to his ability, that is, in accordance with his "design"—his natural capacity and potential as known by the master. Though the proportion given to each servant differed, the master held the same expectation of faithfulness for each one. Each servant acted quickly (whether correctly or incorrectly) upon receiving the talents. Notice the reward given to those who demonstrated faithfulness in their stewardship, as well as the punishment for the one who was "wicked and lazy."

  - What does this parable suggest in relation to gifts, stewardship, and persons with disability?

  - Whose interest was at the forefront of the actions by the faithful servants?

  - What insights do you gain from this parable that can inform your disability ministry?

D. Vulnerability and Power in Weakness

In the previous chapter, I noted that God values our weakness because it is through our weakness that his power can be displayed. Reference was made to Paul's experience (2 Corinthians 12:7–10), which led him to assert that there is power in powerlessness. Paul spoke of his "thorn in the flesh," sent as a messenger of Satan to weaken him but perceived as a gift from God to prevent conceit and boasting in his own strength or accomplishment. Paul did not identify the nature of his "thorn." He simply described it as a weakness or a handicapping condition, something which he found distressing, limiting, perhaps even painful. Three times he asked God to remove this disabling condition. But rather than removing the problem, God gave Paul grace *in* the problem, saying that through his weakness God's strength can be more fully displayed: "My grace is sufficient for you, for my power is made perfect in weakness" (2 Corinthians 12:9).

This transformed how Paul saw his limitation and led him to "boast" in his weakness, allowing God to receive the glory.

Human weakness and God's strength is a theme that runs through the Scriptures. Take David, for example: The youngest (smallest) child of Jesse; from Bethlehem, an historically important town in Israel's history, but insignificant economically; a lad about 10–15 years old who spent his days shepherding sheep and chasing wild animals; seemingly unfit even in the eyes of his father who had not invited him to join the family when Samuel was preparing the sacrifice. Yet is was David that God used, even in—or perhaps because of—his youth to defeat Goliath (1 Samuel 17:40–50).

There were others whose weakness became opportunities for God to display his power: Abraham and Sarah who remained faithful to God's promise of innumerable descendants despite being childless well into old age (Genesis 12:2, 15:5–6, 17:5–6, 17); Joseph, a young and perhaps presumptuous youth whom God raised to the position of prime minister of Egypt (Genesis 37, 39–50); Moses, who argued ineloquence and slowness of speech as an excuse against serving as God's spokesman in Egypt (Exodus 4:10); Gideon, called by God a "mighty man" but who saw himself as the weakest of the weak (Judges 6:11–16); Mary, a young unwed maiden chosen by God to be the one to give birth to the Savior (Luke 1:26–38); Jesus's disciples, ordinary men who "turned the world upside down" (Acts 17:6). Beates concluded that "God's story in Scripture uses these characters to highlight their weakness, their inability, their brokenness. And in so doing, God's glory and God's grace are magnified all the more!" (Beates, 2012, p. 25). Clearly, God chooses unlikely candidates to accomplish his will. We need to learn the lesson which God gave to Samuel. Samuel looked upon the sons of Jesse and was distracted by their appearance and stature—handsome, physically well-built, radiating an air of power. But God told Samuel, "the LORD sees not as man sees: man looks on the outward appearance, but the LORD looks on the heart" (1 Samuel 16:7). We may look upon a person with severe disability and see weakness and limitation. But these are all external characteristics; we cannot see the heart. We must guard against placing restrictions on God's ability to work in and through a person who is "little" by human standards.

Paul's realization that his disability was a gift from God that allowed God's power and glory to be manifest corresponds to what Jesus said to his disciples regarding the man who was born without sight (John 9). Their question exposed typical Jewish thinking, still common among many today: "who sinned, this man or his parents, that he was born blind?" (John 9:2). Jesus explained that sin had no bearing on the man's condition; rather, his blindness was an opportunity for the works of God to be displayed in him (John 9:3).

The fact that God's power is displayed in weakness brings encouragement in the face of our limitations. We rely on God, not on our own energy, effort, or talent. To admit our weakness is to affirm God's strength. And this is as God would have it. What the world considers weak and insignificant is exactly what God wants to use, so that the glory goes to him, not us. God is a jealous God and will not share his glory with anyone or anything (Exodus 34:14; Deuteronomy 4:24; Isaiah 42:8). In our weakness, limitation, or disability, God's greatness, power, and might become manifest. Disability, then, increases our awareness of the sustaining power of God.

This reasoning seems counterintuitive, but it is entirely biblical in that it recognizes the sovereignty of God and acknowledges that his ways are beyond our understanding. Because God cannot contravene his own nature, whatever he does is righteous: "He is like a rock; what he does is perfect, and he is always fair. He is a faithful God who does no wrong, who is right and fair" (Deuteronomy 32:4, NCV). Psalm 148:10 adds that God's right hand is full of righteousness or goodness. We are assured, therefore, that if God includes disability in an individual's design, or allows an accident or illness that results in a disability, or does not answer as we might like when we pray for a cure of a person's disability or disease, *God is still acting righteously.*

The experience of disability is part of the "collective human experience" (Fritzen, 2011, p. 29). Our view of what is healthy and good, or unhealthy and not good, is challenged by disability. But just as the tides ebb and flow, rise and fall, so our life is a series of highs and lows, pleasure and pain, struggle and ease. Disability is often feared because it can make us dependent on others—the more severe the disability, the more dependent we may be. But our independence is more illusory than real: we are born helpless and dependent and we often end our lives in dependence on others, and there is no time when we are not dependent upon God for the very breath of life. Disability reminds us that we are not fully independent, but *interdependent* (more will be said on this in chapter four). No matter how dependent on others a person becomes, being made in the image of God carries with it sanctity and dignity, requiring that we respect and honor others and forbidding any form of discrimination or exploitation. Because people, no matter how disabled, bear the image of God it is inconceivable that we should close our hearts to anyone who is suffering, poor, or marginalized (Dunavant, 2012).

In creating Adam and Eve with a free will, there is a sense in which God himself became vulnerable—vulnerable to being rejected, cursed, even hated by humankind. But God's choice to become vulnerable was done willingly (since, being God, he knew what Adam and Eve would do when tempted by the serpent). In his incarnation, Jesus also became vulnerable, even to the point of death. Again, Jesus did this voluntarily, out of love. In a sense, therefore, our vulnerability is part of being in the image of God. There is no difference between people who are disabled and people who are temporarily able-bodied: "every human life has its limitations, vulnerabilities, and weaknesses We are born needy, and we die helpless. So in truth there is no such thing as a life without disabilities" (Moltmann, 1998, p. 110). Calvary, however, assures us that even the weakest, most vulnerable persons are valued by God. Lane concluded, "The God of Scripture is equally revealed in vulnerability and in triumph . . . . In biblical faith, therefore, brokenness is never celebrated as an end in itself. *God's* brokenness is but an expression of a love on its way to completion" (Lane, 1990 p. 1069, emphasis in the original.)

Though as created beings we are vulnerable, God's power is best displayed through our weakness. Paul stated without reservation that "the weakness of God is stronger than men" (1 Corinthians 1:25). This means that a disability, whether our own or that of someone we know, bankrupts us. It causes us to recognize our dependence upon God as our source of strength, joy, and purpose. It releases us to God, and to the realization that he is our sufficiency. We often attempt to shape God in our own image or likeness rather than acknowledge that God is infinitely greater than what we imagine him to be; his ways are beyond our comprehension (Isaiah 55:8–9). Marva Dawn (2001) suggested that we often miss important details from Scripture or from life experience because we try to understand things according to our human and limited reasoning. She commented, "Even as Jesus was not often understood by his disciples because he worked out of vulnerability and weakness, submitting to suffering and death, so God's ways are often strange, hidden, wild" (p. 8). But Paul affirmed God's ability to bring good out of what we perceive as bad (Romans 8:28). God is not limited by a person's disability; rather, he is able to use our weakness or disability far more than any strength or ability we possess. Joseph's story (Genesis 37–50) attest to God's ability to use undesirable or evil events to bring glory to himself (Genesis 50:20). Richards referred to this as God's ability to "redeem" our experiences, and asserted:

> Although God permits suffering [or disability], he is capable of redeeming any experience, displaying in the life of ill [or disabled] persons his own wondrous working. Sometimes God's work is displayed in healing, for God is the source of health and wholeness; at other times it is displayed through sickness, as he enriches the sufferer and enables him or her to endure in a spirit of praise. (Richards, 1999, p. 565)

A modern-day example is Joni Eareckson Tada, whom God has used to bring encouragement and blessing to persons with disabilities in many counties around the world despite her becoming quadriplegic as a result of a diving accident at age 17. God is able to teach much about himself to and through persons who are disabled, such as grace, patience, love, kindness, and gentleness. Jesus spoke of having a servant attitude (Matthew 20:26–28; Mark 9:35), and Paul admonished believers to demonstrate the same humble servant attitude as Jesus (Philippians 2:3–7). God provides opportunity for us to serve others through our interaction with people who are disabled. God provides occasions when both temporarily able-bodied and disabled persons can become the hands and feet of Jesus reaching out in ministry to others.

When considering the tension between people's antipathy toward weakness and disability and the view embraced by Scripture, Beates concluded:

> Our culture says, "Avoid the broken and the disabled. Hide your weakness and blemishes. Act as if they simply aren't there." But the Scriptures give story after story and proposition after proposition saying instead, "Understand that you—all of you in some sense or another—are broken. Stop avoiding the truth and embrace it." For in that embrace we begin to grasp the power of God through his grace made manifest in human weakness (Beates, 2012, p. 72).

For Further Reflection:

Paul said much that can alter the way persons who are disabled are viewed. Meditate on these passages from the perspective of disability:

1 Corinthians 1:18–31

- Why has God chosen foolish, weak, lowly, and despised things to nullify the powerful, noble, wise, and strong?

- Is it possible that people with disabilities, because they are more openly vulnerable, better "image" God than people who are able-bodied?

- What difference does it make in your life to know that God chooses the weak and lowly people of the world to do His work?

- What do you conclude from this passage about God's character and values?

2 Corinthians 12:1–10

- How does this perspective on power and weakness differ from the perspective of the world?

- What weaknesses, handicaps, or problems in your life is God able to use? How are you encouraged by this passage?

E. Suffering

"Suffering," like poverty, is a relative term. For example, people in the United States who earn a minimum wage salary, may think of themselves as suffering from poverty. Yet for people living in much of the world, to earn that same annual salary might lead them to feel wealthy. Having a disability does not necessarily mean the individual "suffers" as that term is usually used, that is, in the sense of experiencing physical pain. Some physical and health impairments may involve chronic pain, but most disabling conditions do not involve pain-related suffering, except as the individual experiences rejection from others, resulting in exclusion, isolation, or outright abuse. An individual who becomes disabled may experience emotional distress by focusing on what is "lost" because of disability, but this is more related to mental and spiritual outlook than the actual disability, as well as to how they are viewed and treated by others.

When we experience difficult times, such as the birth of a child who is disabled or becoming disabled as a result of injury or illness, it is human nature to ask *"why?"* Because we like to think we are in control of our lives, these events are disturbing—even for Christians, who sometimes mistakenly think they should be immune from any kind of suffering. We find the question "why?" being raised in different ways throughout the Scriptures—Job 30:20; Habakkuk 1:2–4; Psalm 44:23–24, and 88:1, 14, for example. As Christians, we know that God is sovereign and that his grace and mercy to us never cease, but "there are times when our pain is so deep that truths in our mind just can't seem to penetrate the darkness that surrounds our heart" (Shramek, 2006, p. 184). Suffering—our own or that of a loved one—becomes a challenge to our faith and our understanding of God's wisdom. In chapter eight we will consider some theological/philosophical answers to why evil and suffering exist. Here, we will look briefly as five major benefits to suffering suggested by Tada and Bundy (2011, pp. 99–102).

Suffering can lead us and others to Christ. A well-know quote from C. S. Lewis (1962) says "God whispers to us in our pleasures, speaks to us in our conscience, but shouts to us in our pains: it is God's megaphone to rouse a deaf world" (p. 93). Through suffering, God removes any thought of self-sufficiency or self-dependence and convinces us of our need for God (Powlison, 2006). And, through the witness of a Christian's response to suffering, God can lead others to faith. The world is watching believers to see how they respond to pain and suffering. There have been many persons throughout history who bear witness to how God used pain, sorrow, and suffering to bring others to Christ.

Suffering cultivates brokenness and dependence on God. Brokenness (humility) is a prerequisite to following God. Jesus said in Luke 9:23, "If anyone would come after me, let him deny himself and take up his cross daily and follow me." Note that Jesus said this is to be daily, not a one-time experience. For the Christian, brokenness is a way of life. But God comes near to those who are broken and recognize their need for him—"God opposes the proud, but gives grace to the humble" (James 4:6). In Christ, we need not fear our weakness or brokenness because in them, we, like Paul, discover the sufficiency of Christ (2 Corinthians 1:9, 12:9). As Kathy Medina, mother of a child with autism, wisely reminded us, "Just because the trial is bigger than me does not mean that the trial is too big for God" (2006, p. 35).

Suffering transforms us into the likeness of Christ. God intends to transform us into the image of his Son (Romans 8:29; Colossians 3:10; 1 John 3:2). Paul knew that nothing could remove his earthly desires and transform him the way suffering could. Hence, he desired to know the power of Jesus's resurrection and the fellowship of his sufferings (Philippians 3:10). Paul rejoiced in his sufferings because of the benefit received (Romans 5:3–4). A Christian's suffering is part of our call to participate in the humiliation of Christ, just as we will participate in Christ's exaltation (Romans 8:17; cf. James 4:10, 1 Peter 5:6). We do not get to be like Christ without suffering; because Christ suffered, Christians should expect to suffer also. A Christian's suffering for Christ gives witness to the perfect Suffering Servant of God (Isaiah 52:13–53:12). Sproul (1988) suggested that our suffering must be understood as part of God's total plan to "redeem the world through the pathway of suffering" (pp. 39–40). However, it is not sufficient simply to agree that suffering helps transform us into the image of Christ, lest we merely offer people dealing with disability empty words of encouragement, but provide neither needed assistance nor our supportive presence. Nancy Eiesland (2011) said, "I was told that God gave me a disability to develop my character. But by the age of six or seven, I was convinced that I had enough character to last a lifetime" (p. 19). It is not suffering per se that develops us; suffering is merely the catalyst.

Spiritual development comes as we respond properly to suffering or trials. This spiritual maturation is demonstrated in an increased recognition of God's ongoing love and presence, a deepened awareness of our dependence upon God, and an increased thankfulness even in the midst of suffering. These more easily result when believers are genuinely supportive of those in need (cf. James 2:15–16; Colossians 3:12–13).

We, the Church, must be present to those who are in need. We must enter into their "life space" as best we can and provide whatever support we can to persons and families affected by disability. But we must also speak to the society and culture on behalf of those affected by disability—speak verbally, but also speak by demonstrating compassion.

Suffering teaches us compassion for others. Suffering unites Christians with Christ, whose suffering was on our behalf and demonstrated fully the servant attitude which we are to have (Philippians 2:6–8). Our vulnerability and weakness becomes a point of identification with Christ. Our personal suffering, as has already been said, is beneficial to our spiritual development. But it also enables us to minister to others, even out of our weakness (or disability). Paul was clear in stating that the comfort we receive from God is to flow through us as we comfort others (2 Corinthians 1:3–4). Just as God's love is to flow through believers to others, so is God's comfort (technically, also an aspect of his love).

Suffering helps us maintain an eternal perspective. Suffering helps us not to be overly focused on the things of this world, which are temporary. We often become caught up in the worldly affairs and forget that our present circumstances—positive or negative—do not compare to what lies before us in heaven, our final and true home. God's love does not always deliver us from affliction (or disability), but it does sustain us in the midst of our troubles. Patterson (1998) gave this reminder: "Though we have a vision and hope for a fully resurrected future . . . our bodies live now in God's story, which is partial and unfinished" (p. 130). We are participants in God's restoration of all creation (cf. Romans 8:22–24), but since that restoration is not yet completed, we experience weakness, turmoil, the potential of disability, and, ultimately, death. We must learn to be thankful for these reminders, sometimes coming directly from God, that this world is not our home. Warrington (2006) observed that because suffering is inextricably linked to life, Christians are not exempt from it, and cautioned, "It is to be remembered that suffering is an earthbound condition and the Spirit's involvement in the suffering of the believer is certain, and is motivated by love" (p. 162).

Ravi Zacharias (1998) illustrated from the story of Job that the answer to the issues of suffering is relational more than propositional. Rather than give Job an explanation "why" he was suffering, God revealed something of his character as Creator and Designer, Revealer and Comforter, Mediator and Savior, Strengthener and Restorer. Perhaps the greatest lesson to be learned from the story of Job is that "God is not just the God of power in creation; He is the God of presence in our affliction" (Zacharias, p. 83).

Despite having a severe disability, Christopher Newell, formerly Associate Professor in the School of Medicine, University of Tasmania, lectured and wrote on issues of bioethics, disability, and theology. In one of the last things he wrote, he spoke of the importance of brokenness and suffering:

> For me, suffering is crucial to the narration of what it is to be a Christian because, within the broken incarnate God, I find the particular attributes essential for upholding and embracing my life and making sense of my complex journey. In particular, the centrality of the suffering of Jesus—not just in persecution during his life, death, and resurrection but also in his experience of being other—means that I can relate in a very intimate way to a very human God.
>
> Therefore, I have come to reflect that there is an important role for suffering in shaping an authentically lived and experienced good life. My dependence on a variety of people of good will that I have never met is required every day. It requires me to swallow my pride . . . . Yet it has led me to suggest that disability is a deeply important spiritual adventure. (Newell, 2010, pp. 177–178)

For Further Reflection:

What do these verses suggest regarding potential benefits of "suffering" for believers?

- 1 Peter 1:5–7

- James 1:2–4

- Romans 5:3–4

- Romans 8:28–30

- Philippians 2:5–11

Study 2 Corinthians 1:3–11 as a way of understanding God's purposes in our painful experiences. Complete the following thoughts:

- 1:3 Difficult times can help us to know God as . . .

- 1:4–7 Difficult times prepare us to . . .

- 1:8–9 Difficult times teach us to . . .

- 1:10 Difficult times give us . . .

Going Deeper

1. Meditate on Psalm 115. If you can, read from a good commentary what others say about this psalm. Note the crucial teaching of verse 3: "Our God is in the heavens; he does all that he pleases" (ESV). Eugene Peterson, author of *The Message,* paraphrases the verse this way: "Our God is in heaven doing whatever he wants to do" (MSG). Now suppose that you, or someone you know, is dealing with disability—perhaps prenatal testing suggests that the unborn child may have an impairment, or they have given birth to an infant with an obvious disability, or someone in the family has become disabled as the result of an accident or illness. This situation might cause questions to arise in a person's heart like that of Psalm 115:2—*Where is God?*

   a. How can you use this Psalm to bring comfort and encouragement? Some might interpret Psalm 115:3 as meaning that God is a tyrant or autocrat, just doing as he pleases without regard to the consequences or to the people affected. How can you counter that argument?

   b. What does it mean to say God does what he pleases? How can our disability or suffering "please" God? How does this connect with Scripture passages that teach that God is loving and compassionate, that God is "good"?

   c. What is the psalmist trying to communicate about the character of God?

   d. What does the psalm reveal about "who" God is in relationship to his people? What contrast is made between Jehovah God and the idols that others worship?

   e. Times of suffering or difficulty may cause us to feel that God has moved away from us. What Scriptures can you use to assure a person dealing with an impairment and disability of someone in their family of God's love and presence?

   f. Philip Yancey (1990), in recounting some of Joni Eareckson Tada's story, stated the Joni refers to the diving accident that left her a quadriplegic as a "glorious intruder"—words that echo Paul's view of his thorn in the flesh as a gift from God (2 Corinthians 12:7). Joni says that her accident is the best thing that ever happened to her; it was God's way of getting her attention and turning her thoughts toward him, rather than the fleeting things of this world. How does Psalm 115:3 support Joni's perception of her disability-producing accident?

2. Which of the biblical themes regarding the nature of humankind did you find most reassuring? Why?

3. Which, if any, of the biblical themes did you find confusing? What can you do to learn more about that issue?

Chapter Four

Aspects of Ministry

Theme: Characteristics of Ministry

A. The Motivation for Ministry

As with all aspects of Christian ministry, concern for people with disabilities is motivated by love for God, and demonstrated by obedience to Jesus's commission to bring the good news of the gospel to all peoples. The Great Commission found in Matthew 28:18–20 is well known, but often not personally applied. Many Christians wrongly think this command applies only to those called to be career missionaries and, not sensing such a call in their lives, set aside the command. But Jesus's commission, given to every follower of Christ, is not *go*. The main verb (command) of the verse is *make disciples*—the "going" is assumed. We can understand Jesus to be saying "*as you are going about in the world* (walking, living, going one's way, working), *make disciples*." *All* Christians are expected to share the message of salvation and lead others to become disciples—not just making converts, but leading people to become fellow-students or apprentices of Jesus. Every true disciple of Christ, regardless of his or her vocational calling, is to be involved in sharing the gospel wherever they are, through their verbal testimony and their life-witness.

As was noted in chapter one, people with disabilities comprise the largest category of unreached people in the world. Jesus's instruction to make disciples of all peoples thus provides impetus for ministry to people with disabilities. As long as the Church of Christ continues to ignore people affected by disability, the great commission will go unfulfilled.

The ultimate motivation for ministry is that God will be glorified through the lives of all those who are touched with the truth of the gospel. But it is instructive to note that Jesus attached a promise of blessing to our work, especially as it related to people with disabilities. In Luke 14, Jesus commented to his host that to invite to a party those who will simply reciprocate by inviting them to their own banquet leads to limited and earthly reward (14:12). But inviting those who are unable to repay—the poor, the crippled, the lame, or the blind—will lead to blessing (14:13–14). The point is that such hospitality must be demonstrated out of Godlike compassion and love; not out of obligation or self-interest, but solely for God's sake and in God's name. The result will be that God becomes our "debtor" and will repay us at the resurrection. But many who have shown compassion and love to persons with disabilities, and have entered into a relationship with them, will confess that they have already been blessed through that relationship.

For Further Reflection:

The Matthew passage is what most people think of as the "Great Commission," but each Gospel and the Book of Acts contain a version of the command. Study these verses and consider what they reveal about the mission of every Christian. To whom are we to go? What is the content of our message?

1. Matthew 28:18–20

2. Mark 16:15

3. Luke 24:56–48

4. John 20:21

5. Acts 1:8

What have you done to fulfill Jesus's command?

B. Gospel of Compassion and Restoration

To proclaim the gospel is not simply to present the message verbally; we are to make the message of the gospel *visible* in the world. Jesus said, "As the Father has sent me, even so I am sending you" (John 20:21). I understand this to mean more than simply "because I was sent, you are sent." It means we are sent *in the same way* as Jesus was sent: *incarnationally*. Through his incarnation, Jesus entered fully into human existence and identified completely with humankind, even to the point of dying on the cross (Philippians 2:8). As Jesus entered into our world, so we must "enter into" the world of those around us—not just those who are like us, but all who are in need of the message of grace and restoration that Jesus brought. This does not, of course, mean we must become disabled in order to minister to people with disabilities. But we must not exclude them from our focus, nor consider ourselves "better" than they (cf. Philippians 2:3–4).

We are to share the good news in the same manner as Jesus: through words and deeds; through compassion and a call for social justice; through acceptance and welcoming of all people. As Jesus began his ministry, he read from Isaiah 61:1–2 while in the synagogue of Nazareth, giving what we might call his mission statement:

> The Spirit of the Lord is upon me, because he has anointed me to proclaim good news to the poor. He has sent me to proclaim liberty to the captives and recovering of sight to the blind, to set at liberty those who are oppressed, to proclaim the year of the Lord's favor . . . . Then he began to speak to them. "The Scripture you've just heard has been fulfilled this very day!" (Luke 4:18–21)

Those hearing Jesus understood Isaiah's reference to the Year of Jubilee and the restoration it promised (cf. Leviticus 25:10–11). Jesus was instituting the *true* year of Jubilee by proclaiming good news, freedom, recovery, and release. His miracles and welcoming of those oppressed or neglected by society gave evidence that the Jubilee Year had begun: God was in the process of restoring things to the way they were originally intended, especially restoring relationship with himself and with one another—good news indeed for all who accept Jesus and his message. The all-important element of this restoration is Jesus's paying the penalty for sin through his death on the cross, enabling God the Father to justly forgive sinners who accept this free gift and enter into a personal relationship with Christ.

When the authors of the Epistles refer to "the gospel," their clear focus is on the saving work of Christ. In a technical sense, *gospel* refers to "the sum total of saving truth about Jesus as it is communicated to lost humanity" (Richards, 1999, p. 316). But from the teaching and ministry of Jesus, it is evident that we restrict the good news of the gospel if we limit it only to "repent and believe." Jesus proclaimed the good news that God's kingdom is at hand, and his actions showed signs of the restoration promised in the Jubilee: forgiving sins, curing people of disability, honoring widows, receiving and healing lepers, breaking down barriers, restoring some to life. We may conclude that _THE_ *Gospel* is the saving work of Christ on the cross, but the _MESSAGE_ *of the gospel* speaks more to the results of our redemption which grow from the Jubilee restoration; that is, the victorious, spiritually healing, liberating, and reconciling work which God accomplished in Christ. The good news does not have to wait until heaven to be good news!

> [B]eing a Christian, a follower of Jesus Christ, requires much more than just having a *personal* and transforming relationship with God. It also entails a *public* and transforming relationship with the world . . . . The gospel itself was born of God's vision of a changed people, challenging and transforming the prevailing values and practices of our world. (Stearns, 2010, p. 2, emphasis in the original.)

The kingdom of which Christ spoke was one in which the poor, the sick, the grieving, cripples, slaves, women, children, widows, orphans, lepers, and aliens—the "least of these" (Matthew 25:40)—were to be lifted up and embraced by God. It was a world order in which justice was to become a reality, first in the hearts and minds of Jesus's followers, and then to the wider society through their influence. (Stearns, 2010, p. 16)

The effect of this is that the message we bring today should not just be heard in our words, but seen in compassionate ministry with those in need. As we minister to and with persons who are disabled, we seek to bring them into relationship with God and with the entire community of faith by breaking barriers which separate people. Paul wrote, "there is no Greek or Jew, circumcised or uncircumcised, barbarian, Scythian, slave or free, but Christ is all, and is in all" (Colossians 3:11). Paul's point was that Christ assimilates within himself all differences—all humankind is God's creation; Christ's blood was shed equally for all. We do no violence to God's Word by extending Paul's comment to include "there is no disabled or non disabled."

God's Word has a clear focus on social justice and compassion as reflections of God's character. The Old Testament prophets in particular declared God's concern for those who were looked down upon or pushed aside by society—the poor, widows, orphans, foreigners. This theme was extended and broadened in the ministry of Jesus to include people marginalized because of disability. Paul urged Christians to have the same attitude as Jesus (Philippians 2:5), which requires an expression of compassion and a desire to serve others, including those with significant needs related to a disability. For Christians, this service and compassion goes beyond humanistic or democratic ideals, recognizing the strong scriptural foundation for social justice and equality grounded in the doctrine of God and the nature of humankind.

Jesus is the embodiment of God's love (John 3:16). Our being sent as the Father sent Jesus demands that we also embody the love and compassion of God, who abounds in love and faithfulness (Psalm 86:15) and is slow to anger but rich in love (Psalm 145:8). Just as Jesus responded with love and compassion to people who were harassed and helpless (Matthew 9:36), bringing them words of love and spiritual healing (Matthew 14:14; Matthew 20:24), so must we.

> Jesus invited all of his followers, including any of us today who believe in him, to participate in the kingdom as its agents, witnesses, and models . . . . [T]o be a "Christ person" is to be a "kingdom person." Working in that kingdom is our way of life. (Plantinga, 2002, p. 107)

To say that Christians are the "Body of Christ" (1 Corinthians 12:27; Ephesians 4:12) does not simply mean we are spiritually united with him. It means we are the location of Christ's ongoing ministry in the world today. All ministry requires embodiment and action; for our ministry to be incarnational requires that we enter into the "world" of those we serve—in our case, people with disabilities and their families. It means serving them, walking alongside them as it were, just as Christ served and walked alongside his disciples and others in his earthly ministry. It means modeling the principle behind Paul's statement, "I have made myself a servant to all, that I might win more of them" (1 Corinthians 9:19).

God's people are "to be the voice of the voiceless and the champion of the powerless" (Stott, 1990, p. 157). Like the prophets of old, we are to speak God's truth into situations where injustice is widespread and culturally systemic. The prophets often spoke on behalf of the weakest and most vulnerable in their community, taking a public stance against the injustice they endured, whether that injustice was out of ignorance or intentional disregard. Like the prophets, the Church must call for justice on behalf of all who experience injustice for any reason—in our focus, people with disabilities who have been pushed aside through ignorance or social policy.

For Further Reflection:

What timeless principle is taught in the following verses? What do they suggest as ways of showing compassion to people and families affected by disability?

- 1 Peter 3:8–10

- 1 John 3:17–18

- James 2:15–20

- Romans 12:15–18

C. Hospitality

Biblical hospitality is a rich concept that holds particular theological and practical significance for disability ministry. Old Testament narratives demonstrating the practice of hospitality include Genesis 18 and 19, where strangers are entertained by Abraham and Lot, respectively; 1 Kings 17, where the widow of Zarephath hosts Elijah; and 2 Kings 4, the story of Elisha and the Shunammite woman. The hospitality offered included housing and shelter, washing the guests' feet, providing a meal, and provision of a safe environment, but my focus here is on the *posture*, not the *form* of hospitality.

Two of Jesus's parables especially emphasized hospitality. In the parable of the sheep and goats (Matthew 25:31–46), Jesus explained the "kingdom mandate of ministry, which is to serve human needs without respect of persons" (Sanders, 1997, p. 27). Everyday acts of mercy toward people who are strangers, hungry, in prison, poor, diseased, or disabled are mentioned—acts that every Christian can perform regardless of economic status, intellectual level, or degree of able-bodiedness. Throughout his ministry, Jesus demonstrated hospitality as he welcomed individuals with various needs and life-situations. The second notable parable is that of the great banquet (Luke 14:16–23). The invited guests rudely refuse to come, so their place is given to the poor, crippled, blind, and lame living in the city streets and alleys and in the country lanes. Taken together, these two parables demonstrate the distinctiveness of Christian hospitality: the possibility that in welcoming "the least" we may actually be welcoming Jesus, and an orientation toward those who have little to offer by way of reciprocity. Pohl noted that these passages "tie human responsibility to God's welcome, and God's presence and reward to simple acts of care (Pohl, 2003, p. 8).

Biblical hospitality is evident in God's concern for justice, particularly for those who tend to be marginalized: aliens and strangers, the poor, widows, orphans, the diseased and disabled. It is also seen in Jesus's crossing barriers of religion, ethnicity, gender, ability level, and other walls of separation erected by the culture. From Jesus's parable of the good Samaritan (Luke 10:25–37) we learn that when we come upon someone in need, rather than avoiding the person, we are to make ourselves neighbor to that man or woman. The parable depicts how hospitality should be evidenced in the life of a Christian, and further illustrates crossing artificial barriers that are often erected.

Hospitality was an important witness to the authenticity of the gospel during the early centuries of the Christian era. The Greek word translated as "hospitality" or "hospitable" (*philoxenia*) means fond of strangers or guests. The apostle Paul instructed Christians to "practice hospitality" (Romans 12:13) and listed being hospitable among the qualifications for church leaders (1 Timothy 3:2, 5:10; Titus 1:8). The author of Hebrews charged readers not to neglect showing hospitality to strangers, reminding them that by so doing, some have entertained angels without knowing it (Hebrews 13:2). Peter spoke of hospitality within the context of loving and serving others so as to bring glory and praise to God (1 Peter 4:8–11).

Theologically, Christian hospitality is significant because it recognizes and images *God's* acts of hospitality. The descendants of Abraham, living as aliens in bondage to Egypt, were a people whom God graciously redeemed and constituted as a nation. During their wanderings in the wilderness, hospitality to Israel was shown in God's provision of food and water, and protection from their enemies. God's covenant with Israel included a code of hospitality (Exodus 22:21; Leviticus 19:9–10, 33–34) based on God's holiness and graciousness (Leviticus 19:1–2). This became a reminder of God's faithful provision of safety and sustenance during their wilderness experience. Christ's atoning work, through which our alienation from God is removed, is the extreme example of God's offer of hospitality. The metaphor of *embrace* used by Volf pictures hospitality. To Volf, hospitality means a willingness to make space for others, just as "on the cross, God made space in God's very self for others . . . and opened arms to invite them in" (1996, p. 214).

Hospitality requires "the creation of a free and friendly space where we can reach out to strangers and invite them to become our friends" (Nouwen, 1975, p. 79). Reinders cautioned, however, that "Space is a *necessary* but not a *sufficient* condition for inclusion" (2008, p. 161). The hospitality envisioned is an intentional practice that reflects a process and perspective rather than specific tasks. As Reynolds (2008) explained, "Hospitality embodies divine love, it neither condescends out of pity nor forces the other to conform . . . but rather lets the other be, yielding space for the others' freedom and difference" (p. 241). Hospitality is offered freely and openly. True hospitality is an openness and sharing with one another.

While an individual's impairment, and the functional limitations it may cause, must not be ignored, hospitality demands that each person be seen as an individual created in God's image. The cognitive, affective, or physical/sensory impairment obviously presents some limitation, but this is only one aspect of the person, not the totality of his or her being. Pohl's comment about biblical hospitality shows its relationship to reconciliation and interdependence:

> Hospitality practices that offer a transforming social network to detached strangers require a heterogeneous community with multiple intersecting relationships and fluid roles . . . . Without reciprocal relations and commitments, without hosts and guests aware of their need and dependence on one another, relations are flattened and commitments are too thin to give people a place in the world. (Pohl, 1995, pp. 134–135)

Biblical accounts of hospitality focused on entertaining strangers or aliens, people who were vulnerable because of being "outsiders," and potentially victims of abuse, either overtly (as in the case of the man who fell among thieves in Jesus's parable of the good Samaritan) or covertly (as in the intentional disregard of that unfortunate man by the priest and Levite who passed him by). Individuals and families affected by disability may similarly be seen as outsiders, thus being vulnerable to isolation or discrimination. Attitudinal barriers built from fear or ignorance often result in the person with a disability not being acknowledged as a true peer by those who are temporarily able-bodied.

Christian hospitality builds on mutual respect, acknowledging that the "guest" also brings something to the relationship. This can promote friendships and solidarity by enabling temporarily able-bodied persons and those with disabilities to see themselves as equals despite obvious differences in ability. The biblical principle of loving others as you love yourself suggests an appreciation for this equality.

The Gospel calls Christians to be obedient servants of Christ and show the same concern for justice and compassion as Jesus did, recalling the words of Micah 6:8, "what does the LORD require of you but to do justice, and to love kindness, and to walk humbly with your God?" Through Christian hospitality we mediate the love of Christ to persons: "When we offer hospitality . . . we make a powerful statement to the world about who is interesting, valuable, and important to us" (Pohl, 2003, p. 11). Hospitality should characterize the Christian's life, as our lives are shared with others. "It involves opening our lives to those who need a place, and making room for those the world often overlooks and undervalues" (Pohl & Buck, 2004, p. 11).

For Further Reflection:

- Hospitality can be a means of grace for both the giver and receiver of hospitality. Can hospitality contribute to a person's spiritual formation? How?

- If disabled and able-bodied are given opportunities to practice giving and receiving hospitality, how might that contribute to healing of relationships?

- The morality of a nation can be measured by how it treats its most vulnerable members (Sanders, 1997). Do you agree or disagree with this statement? Why or why not? Can the same be said about the morality of a church?

- "The key to unlocking the door of hospitality is maintaining an open and ready heart" (Reynolds, 2006, p. 201). How "ready" is your heart to show hospitality to people who are affected by disability? How can you help your church to be open?

- By what concrete actions can you show people affected by disability that they are welcome? Are modifications or accommodations needed in your church building or the worship service? How can you show kindness and develop friendships with persons affected by disability?

D. Shalom and Spiritual Warfare

This theme ties together much of what has been said thus far. Shalom often is understood narrowly to mean 'peace' in the sense of the absence of conflict. But biblical shalom is a much richer concept encompassing well-being characterized by right, or harmonious, relationships with God, oneself, others, and all of creation. Plantinga (2002) described biblical shalom as a "universal flourishing, wholeness, and delight—a rich state of affairs in which natural needs are satisfied and natural gifts fruitfully employed, all under the arch of God's love" (p. 15). The wholeness and completeness which God intended at creation characterizes shalom. In the Psalms and the Prophets, shalom captures the experience of God's presence with his people.

The New Testament equivalent of shalom (*eirene*), carries a similar richness of meaning, especially connoting restoration and relationship as all that separates people from God and from one another is replaced with unity in and through Christ (cf. Ephesians 2:14–17; 1 Corinthians 14:33; Colossians 3:12–15).

Spiritual warfare, on the other hand, is "that conflict being waged in the invisible, spiritual realm that is being manifest in the visible, physical realm" (Evans, 1998, p. 18). This is warfare in which all humankind is caught up. Its impact can be seen and felt in individual lives, families, culture, and even churches. Satan's basic warfare strategy is deception; the Bible tells us he seeks to deceive the whole world (Revelation 12:9). Satan uses various schemes or methods to deceive (Ephesians 6:11), all with the intent to damage or destroy, but his basic attack is essentially the same as used with Eve: twisting God's words to confuse or delude; questioning the meaning of, or motivation behind God's words; getting people to focus on what they lack, or to ask the often unanswerable question "Why?" Jesus explained that Satan does not stand in the truth, for there is no truth in him (John 8:44). Satan's greatest lie is that God does not care. As he did with Eve, Satan continues to assail God's love, justice, caring, compassion, and integrity. He encourages the mythological and superstitious thinking about disability and disabled persons found among people in developing nations, and often lying beneath the surface in the thoughts of people in more developed nations. He convinces people that weakness is "just the way things are" and causes people to view those with disabilities as insignificant or less than human. Satan can even convince persons with disabilities to see themselves this way, especially in cultures which emphasize strength, ability, achievement, beauty, and youth. Satan would rather our focus remain on the *dis*-ability and limitation caused by the handicapping condition—what the individual cannot do or do well. This keeps individuals who are disabled "bound" in negativity, both by their own self-understanding and by society's view of them as objects to be pitied.

The lies and deception of Satan hold people in captivity. But Jesus brings light and truth, life and freedom. Jesus focused on what God desires: community, reconciliation, interdependence, relationship, and connectedness with God, ourselves, and others. Promoting disability awareness and ministry in churches, enlightening both the able-bodied and those with disabilities to the truths we have been exploring in this book, and empowering people with disabilities, engages us in spiritual warfare—with the goal of freeing the captives and releasing the oppressed (cf. Luke 4:18–20). To destroy the works of the devil is why Jesus came into the world (1 John 3:8). Jesus said that "no one can enter a strong man's house and carry off his possessions unless he first ties up the strong man" (Mark 3:27, NIV). Luke puts even greater emphasis into Jesus's words: "When a strong man, fully armed, guards his own house, his possessions are safe. But when someone stronger attacks and overpowers him, he takes away the armor in which the man trusted and divides up the spoils" (Luke 11:21–22, NIV). Jesus entered the strong man's (Satan's) house, overpowered and bound him, and stripped away his armor and weaponry. As Christians, we are commissioned by the Lord to plunder the strong man's possessions. Ours is a rescue mission authorized by Jesus (Matthew 28:18–20), not simply to "save souls" but to create a God-centered community that offers salvation, physical care, nurturing, economic support, reconciliation, restoration to those in need—in short, shalom. We are charged with breaking down walls that separate people from Christ, from one another, from society, and from becoming "whole" through Christ. Disability ministry seeks to restore people whom society and even families have pushed aside. Our work is with people who have been dispossessed of the truth as to who they are, and who may be convinced that they are worthless, that God does not care or is powerless to help.

The weapons with which we fight are God's weapons (see Ephesians 6:14–18), all wielded with love and compassion in the name of the Lord Jesus Christ. These weapons, brandished through right doctrine and right living, have divine might—literally, they are "mighty through God." The power by which we wage this conflict is not our own, but God's, and through it, we pull down strongholds or fortresses in which people have become entrenched (2 Corinthians 10:4). These strongholds include mindsets that hold people hostage, believing that they are hopelessly locked in a situation, powerless to change; barriers of ignorance, prejudice, stereotype, and misconception as to *disability* and the personal worth of individuals who have disabilities; thought patterns or ideas that cloud people's reasoning, leading some to a self-centered lifestyle, and others to become entrenched in feelings of hopelessness.

We promote shalom by being peacemakers (Matthew 5:9), by being ministers of reconciliation (2 Corinthians 5:18–19), and by promoting interdependence. Other ways in which our behavior as redeemed image bearers should make a difference in our world include seeking healing (overcoming physical illness, psychological suffering, social isolation, etc.); promoting spiritual renewal and a sense of purpose; freeing people from things that hold power over them, such as drugs, poverty, and various forms of oppression; seeking equity and fairness in the way people deal with one another; and dwelling in harmony with God, others, self, and the world. As the people of God, we are called to demonstrate our citizenship in the kingdom of God even as we live in this world, where Satan is still active despite being ultimately defeated through the Cross (1 Corinthians 15:54–57). Richard Mouw wrote about Christian civility in an uncivil world, and stated, "When shalom happens, everything is functioning in the way the Creator intended" (1992, p. 35)

For Further Reflection:

- Examine these scripture verses to identify what they teach about shalom: Numbers 6:26; Psalm 29:11; Isaiah 26:3; John 14:27; Romans 5:1; Galatians 5:22

- Consider these verses and summarize what they teach about the Christian's involvement in spiritual warfare: Ephesians 6:10–18; 2 Corinthians 2:11; Matthew 12:29 (see also Luke 11:21–22)

Theme: Outcomes of Ministry

A. Reconciliation

Christians have been given both the message and the ministry of reconciliation (2 Corinthians 5:18–19). Biblical reconciliation involves a radical change or transformation of a relationship—from a position of enmity to one of friendship and harmony with God and each other. Christian ministry seeks to help people, including those with disabilities, become reconciled to God through Jesus Christ. Christian ministry also involves helping the temporarily able-bodied accept and appreciate people who have disabilities, and recognize the *strengths and abilities* of these persons. Furthermore, Christian ministry seeks to help both able-bodied and disabled individuals to develop their God-given potential. As stated earlier, the Bible's teaching about living and loving; about relationship with God and others; and about sin, grace, and forgiveness is directly relevant to this ministry of reconciliation.

DeYoung (1997) described reconciliation as our greatest challenge and greatest hope. Though he was specifically speaking about racial reconciliation and harmony, his words apply equally to our focus on disability. He identified three roadblocks to the reconciliation we seek to promote: isolation, injustice, and denial. These roadblocks create barriers which "negatively influence our ways of thinking and perceiving" and "affect our ability and willingness to engage in efforts that might lead to reconciliation" (p. 15). These roadblocks grow out of attitudes of superiority on the part of able-boded persons who perceive those with disabilities as weak, limited, abnormal, deviant, or dysfunctional. People affected by handicapping conditions are often seen as being in competition for limited resources (the scarcity paradigm, spoken of in chapter one). The view that disabled individuals are inferior and less worthy results in their continued marginalization. Some contend that people with disabilities should be "put away" somewhere or even exterminated in order to "protect" society. But segregating the disabled also isolates the able-bodied and reinforces a false sense of superiority which DeYoung appropriately perceived to be "a direct challenge to the position of God in the world and a form of self-idolatry. In truth, only God is superior. The rest of us are neither inferior nor superior. We are equally created in the image of God" (p. 18).

Sadly, efforts to promote social justice on behalf of persons with disabilities have not been championed by the Christian church, despite the clear Scriptural declaration of God's concern for—and the extent to which Jesus's ministry embraced—social outcasts, including those with disabilities (e.g., Luke 14:15–24 [Parable of the Great Banquet], Matthew 9:36 [Jesus' compassion on the harassed, helpless, and scattered; i.e., those marginalized by society], and Matthew 25:31–46 ['the least of these my brothers']). Few churches openly welcome persons with disabilities to fellowship with them; many disabled persons feel they are "disinvited" by churches (Webb-Mitchell, 1994b).

The false sense of superiority among temporarily able-bodied persons leads to denial of the full humanity of those who are disabled. The presumption that people with disabilities need pity and charity fosters the idea that they are simply in need of help, and overturns any recognition that we are all created in God's image and that God has given gifts and talents to everyone.

Earlier, I referred to Henri Nouwen's work at L'Arche Daybreak Community in Toronto with a young man named Adam who had a severe disability. Nouwen commented:

> Most people saw Adam as a disabled person who had little to give and who was a burden to his family, his community, and to society at large. And as long as he was seen that way, his truth was hidden. (1997, p. 31)

Nouwen's account described his own reconciliation with Adam. He detailed how his initial fearfulness dissipated as he grew to know Adam to the point where he recognized him as a human being, rather than as a "disability."

Reconciliation is at the core of community, but community does not mean uniformity. Each person is an individual, made in the image of God, and uniquely designed, gifted, and purposed by God. Jean Vanier, founder of a Christian residential program for people with disabilities, concluded that community occurs when each person is seen as unique and as having a gift to offer others. Vanier's exhortation is significant: "We must learn to love difference, to see it as a treasure and not a threat" (Vanier, 1992, p. 44). Without reconciled attitudes, persons with disabilities are easily stripped of their humanity and labeled unworthy, useless, accursed, or less than human. Those who "disable" by labeling and segregating people with handicapping conditions do not realize that in so doing they also lose their own humanity because they act inhumanely. Thus, they also need reconciliation. They need to be liberated from the assumption that they are "healthy" and from their fear of persons with disabilities. When such fears are reduced through increased knowledge and through living in community with persons who are disabled, people will come to appreciate the gifts that these individuals have and are.

Reconciliation has been affirmed as the theological foundation for the Christian faith, but we must move beyond simply accepting it as a theological truth. God committed to us the *message* of reconciliation: that God, in Christ, was reconciling the world to himself (2 Corinthians 5:19). And in committing this message of reconciliation to us, God commissioned us into a *ministry* of reconciliation (2 Corinthians 5:18). We are to actively participate in a ministry whose goal is calling others to reconciliation: with God (Colossians 1:21–22; Romans 5:10); with others (Ephesians 2:16); and with "self" as a new creation (2 Corinthians 5:17). This moves beyond mere evangelism (which emphasizes the reconciling work God completed in Christ), and challenges us to actively seek reconciliation of people across all barriers: racial, class, gender, *and ability*. Indeed, it calls us to the task of bridging or eliminating those barriers.

For Further Reflection:

- Jesus instituted the true year of jubilee as he proclaimed the good news, freedom, and release or liberation to the oppressed. For Jesus, liberation and reconciliation were not abstract concepts; they were to be observed in the lives of the people Jesus touched. Jesus sought people who were seen as lacking something, as outcasts—the same way many people with disabilities are perceived today. How can you (and your church) "be" Jesus in your community, and reach out and promote reconciliation?

- Christ's ministry to people with disabilities was not only a visible sign that the jubilee year had begun, it also attested to the fact that the kingdom of God was present. How can you (and your church) similarly make visible the kingdom of God? What needs to change in your own heart? In your ministry focus?

- As Christ's body, we need to embrace and include in our ministry the same kinds of people Jesus embraced and included. What effect would there be in your community to see you (and your church) reaching out to the broken, sick, disabled, and oppressed as Jesus did?

B. Interdependence

I have already discussed how fear, ignorance, superstition, arrogance, and pride on the part of the able-bodied leads to devaluing or discrediting people with disabling conditions, significantly limiting their opportunities for social interaction. To counter this tendency, Black described a *theology of interdependence* which "honors the value of all individuals, not by what they do, but by who they are, recognizing that each and every person contributes to the community by being, not by doing (Black, 1996, p. 42). This runs counter to notions of independence and self-reliance. It challenges the desire to "be our own person" with scriptural teaching regarding the interdependence of humankind.

Interdependence has been part of God's design from the beginning. Genesis 2 provides insight into the Creator's mind. Adam was free to enjoy the beauty of God's creation including, presumably, romping with the animals. But this would not "complete" the man. God declared

Adam's solitude "not good" and provided a companion perfectly suited to Adam (Genesis 2:18). This does not imply that creating a person to correspond to Adam was an afterthought. The verse is written for *our* benefit—to highlight God's intention that there be an interdependent relationship among human beings. To help Adam realize his need for a suitable companion, God brought all the animals to the man for him to name (Genesis 2:19–20). We can assume the animals came in pairs (male and female) which would help Adam realize his counterpart was missing. God's goal was to show that the man and the woman each needed the other—not out of dependency, where one is superior to the other, but in partnership, as equals who are interdependent in a way that the two become one. After creating Eve, God presented her to Adam as his companion, his face-to-face equal. In response to what God had done, Adam exclaimed, "this at last is bone of my bones and flesh of my flesh" (Genesis 2:23), in recognition of the completeness or wholeness that interdependence brings.

Using the analogy of the human body, Paul recounted our interdependence as members of the body of Christ in 1 Corinthians 12:23–26, describing persons as having different functions, but all belonging to one another: "God has so composed the body, giving greater honor to the part that lacked it, that there may be no division in the body, but that the members may have the same care for one another."

When first encountering a person with obvious disabilities, attention often is focused on the limitation. Rarely is any thought given to what gifts may lie hidden beneath the exterior shell of limitation. Able-bodied persons may experience anxiety, fearing how their life would be impacted if they, or someone they loved, became disabled. Rather than seeing *a person* with a disability, they see a person who has (or "is") *a need*—an object of charity or pity, assuming the primary need is for assistance. Little thought is given to the possibility that the disabled individual has something to offer others. But in truth, no one to truly independent; we all need help at many times in our lives.

My point is that the presence of diversity and difference in our world is typical (recall the discussion of *normal* in chapter one). As with Adam and Eve, God did not create us the same—we are each uniquely made as God's image-bearer to reflect God's glory. A theology of interdependence emphasizes community, but as said earlier, community does not mean uniformity. The Church, as an inclusive community, should be characterized by the recognition and encouragement of the gifts and talents of each individual, including those considered severely disabled.

Community cannot exist without openness to others (Meininger, 2001, p. 19). Relationships and belonging become hallmarks of the type of community the Church needs to establish and to be. Interdependence emphasizes that each part of the community is important to the other. We could say that 'community' is a way of life, a situation in which interconnections are pervasive. Recognition of the reciprocity of interdependence results in appreciation for the abilities and gifts of persons who are disabled and leads us to welcome and celebrate difference. A spirit of reciprocity would then surface in which there is a mutual sense of responsibility to and need of one another—similar to what Paul described as the Body of Christ in 1 Corinthians. When the unique contributions each person makes to the community are recognized and valued, a sense of belonging is fostered. The Church needs to be a place where differences are embraced rather than avoided, where everyone feels safe, connected, and cared for.

The Trinity provides an example of interdependence: three distinct Persons, yet in complete unity. That same unity in diversity is seen in the New Testament description of the church as a community (*koinonia*: fellowship, partnership, communion)—believers from different national, ethnic, and socioeconomic backgrounds, yet one family through Jesus Christ. Paul's teaching about the variety of gifts (spiritual and otherwise) within the church, yet still forming one interconnected and interdependent body, completes the image of unity in diversity. Each member of the body has received different gifts, but they are to be exercised within the "oneness" of the body (Romans 12:5; 1 Corinthians 12:7; Ephesians 4:12). Our dependence upon one another is part of God's design; interdependence is "the core of the very definition of God's people" (Petersen, 1993, p. 34).

For Further Reflection:

- How does your church match the description of an interdependent community described above? What needs to happen to make it a community of belonging for *all* people?

- How does Jesus's teaching, "Blessed are the peacemakers, for they shall be called sons of God" (Matthew 5:9), relate to creating a community in which interrelationship is evident?

- Reconciliation and interdependence are complementary concepts. How does Ephesians 2:11–16 speak to both?

C. Biblical Justice

In chapter one, I spoke of the myth of normalcy, which leads to the assumption that people who are disabled are "not normal" (abnormal). The determination that people who are disabled need to become normal has led to medical, educational, and psychological efforts to prevent disability or to treat disabled persons so that they can function more "normally." But it has led others to overly stress the need for curing through prayer, confession, and anointing with oil. The assumption that people with disabilities need to become "normal" (or even *want* to be "normal") may actually lead to an *injustice*. When miraculous healing does not occur, the individual is often blamed as not having sufficient faith or harboring unconfessed sin, and is often abandoned. (More will be said about this in chapter seven)

Justice is often viewed along the lines of "equality." Hauerwas, however, observed that although people assume that being treated equally is to be treated justly, this is not always the outcome. Instead, the language of equality reduces everyone to a "common denominator that can be repressive or disrespectful . . . No one wants to pay the price of being treated equally if that means they must reject who they are" (Hauerwas, 2004, p. 39).

Many think of justice as a *thing*—a state or a situation; an entitlement. Justice, understood this way, is a *noun* referring to something that resides outside of self. People then become more concerned with their own experience of justice, often at the expense of justice for others. This view allows people to think of justice or human rights as something we accord or withhold depending on what a person does or can do, and how we perceive that individual. Some people even question whether severely disabled individuals are truly "human." If they are not, then the question of justice or human rights is a non-issue. But neither the presence nor absence of disability brings into question the humanness of the individual or that person's creation as the image of God. The fact that all humans are created in the image of God brings a moral obligation never to treat persons as having less worth, never to under-respect persons, never to demean them.

Rather than something external to oneself, biblical justice is more properly understood as a *verb*, an action. Micah 6:8 says, "He has told you, O man, what is good; and what does the LORD require of you but to *do justice*, and to love kindness, and to walk humbly with your God?" (emphasis added). In the biblical context, justice is not simply a *thing we experience;* it is an *action to be performed*. The original Hebrew and Greek words for *justice* and for *righteousness* are essentially the same and are primarily focused on one's relation to others (Orr, 1939). Sanders (1997) put it this way: "Justice is the moral principle that corresponds most closely to the divine attribute of righteousness. In ethical terms, justice is the imperative to do what is right in a manner that is fair and impartial" (p. 15). Contemporary usage of the word, however, limits our understanding of justice, and masks its use in the Bible as a synonym for *righteousness* (Roberts, 2002).

Biblical justice is rooted in the nature and character of God. According to Richards (1999), doing justice has to do with how people treat one another:

> The normal or standard that defines just behavior is a moral and ethical one. It is derived from God's character and is expressed in those commands of the law and expectations of the prophets that reveal how God expects his people to relate lovingly to those around them. (p. 270)

Richards maintained that the biblical concept of justice or righteousness is dynamic, reaching beyond as simple evaluation of a person's behavior to examine the person's character. He concluded that the biblical concept of justice "calls us to love and concern for those who are weak and oppressed, not simply to moral action in our interpersonal dealings" (1999, p. 372).

Micah 6:8 emphasizes *doing justice*, particularly in regard to those who are vulnerable, disadvantaged, or oppressed by the more powerful in society. Justice must be a lifestyle, evidenced by a motivation to practice good and interact in a manner that will establish and maintain just relationships with others. Just as justice/righteousness is grounded in God's nature, that same justice/right behavior must be manifest in Christians. As Christ's representatives we speak for those who may have little or no "voice." We give justice a human form as we speak to both those in need and those who keep people in need. "In the practice of justice, Christians actively take part in the compassionate acts of God" (Zorrilla, 1988, p. 79).

Justice is sometimes thought to be a synonym for *fairness*, "but often God's justice equals not what is fair but what is right" (Ryken, Wilhoit, & Longman, 1998, p. 474). Rather than meaning everyone receives equal treatment, justice means everyone receives what he or she needs (Smart, 2001). The first view stresses *sameness*, denying individuality and disregarding diversity in order to promote uniformity. The second view, a more mature understanding of justice and fairness, implies a shift from an abstract principle-based idea, to a value-based ethic of care, in which benevolence assumes a greater role as consideration is given to individual differences and the needs of others. This view of justice/fairness shows greater accord with the Bible's declaration that God is impartial (cf. Deuteronomy 19:17, Job 34:19, Acts 10:34, Romans 2:11). God's impartiality does not mean that all people are treated alike. It simply means there is no favoritism; all receive what is needed.

When disability, and persons who have a disability, are not understood, and the interdependence of all people not recognized, those with disabilities are easily devalued, dismissed, or set aside as the responsibility of "someone else." Micah 6:8 points the way to correcting this situation. It highlights the connection between justice and love and includes an implied warning against a hierarchical view of people ("walk humbly with your God"). It calls attention to barriers that often exists between the temporarily able-bodied and persons who have a disability, barriers that necessitate reconciliation so that justice can prevail. "To establish justice is to remove anything that hinders healthy relationships between people. To live out justice has to do with resolving conflict so that a community can experience peace and harmony" (Zorrilla, 1998, p. 38).

Lack of harmony necessitates a radical transformation based on principles of biblical justice. The church must become a microcosm of an inclusive community whose effect may eventually be seen in society at large. As with reconciliation, justice is a lifestyle rather than simply a strategy for human relations. Both require a re-envisioning of all persons based on a scriptural understanding of what it means to be human and to be God's image-bearer.

Applying principles of biblical justice and reconciliation, demonstrating love and kindness and walking humbly before God, can result in appreciation for the abilities and gifts of persons with disabilities and encourage welcoming and celebration of difference and the contributions of each member of the community. This can promote a mutual sense both of responsibility to and need of one another—similar to what Paul described as the Body of Christ.

Instead of fostering competition, a just community will provide a common place where members share a common purpose. A true community is "one in which there is a natural, emotional, and interdependent association among people" (Frazee, 2001, p. 200). Biblical justice establishes a situation in which shalom is possible. But neither biblical justice nor shalom are magical formulas apart from individuals.

Just as Jesus broke through barriers of gender, religion, ethnicity, and ability/disability during his earthly ministry, Christians must also challenge practices and ideologies that lead to the exclusion of others. All Christians are to "do what is right to other people, love being kind to others, and live humbly, obeying your God" (Micah 6:8, NCV). We can conclude with Senior (1995), that including persons with disabilities in the social, political, and religious community "is an issue of justice fundamental to the Gospel. Exclusion, on the other hand, has an oppressive, dehumanizing impact running contrary to the Christian vision" (p. 6).

For Further Reflection:

- Tiffany and Ringe (1996, p. 183) asked, "Why is such a premium placed on able-bodiedness? Why is the 'good news' not expressed as a world made accessible to and accepting of persons of all physical, mental, and psychological circumstances, rather than as persons changed to conform to the world's norms?"

  The second question implies that not being conformed to the norm of able-bodiedness makes a person "unacceptable." How do these question relate to biblical justice? How do you answer these questions?

- Simon Horne (1998, p. 97) related this comment made by his wife: "My impairment is genetic, so when I was made, God included my impairment, and I have no problems with that. What I do have problems with is the fact that society disables me. God did not make me to be someone who is disabled by society."

  Her comment points to the fact that it is not her impairment, but society's attitude that disables. Do you consider the implied negative judgment by able-bodied persons an instance of injustice? Why or why not?

- Meditate on Micah 6:8. What does doing justice, loving kindness, and walking humbly with God mean as far as disability ministry is concerned? How have you (and your church) violated this principle? What are some practical steps you (and your church) can take to promote reconciliation, shalom, and justice on behalf of persons with disabilities?

Going Deeper

Reflections on the Biblical Themes:

1. Which biblical theme addressed in thie chapter most speaks to you as you consider your own Christian life and ministry to and with persons who have disabilities?

2. What biblical theme caused confusion or conflict in your understanding of the world and of God? Why? How do you plan to resolve the challenge it made to your thinking?

3. What additional biblical themes can you identify in relation to ministry to and with persons who have disabilities?

4. When you consider the biblical themes discussed in this chapter and the previous chapter, which theme(s) do you need to study more in the biblical narrative?

5. After considering the biblical themes from this and the previous chapter what ideas are developing in your thinking as to how you (and your church) might begin to minister to and with people who are disabled?

Section Three
Making Theology Practical in Ministry

Chapter Five

Designing Ministry to (and with) Persons who are Disabled

"A ministry to the disability community affords the church a wonderful opportunity to display God's magnificent, unconditional, and impartial love before the watching world" (Newman & Tada, 1993, p. 24)

Thomas Reynolds explained that when a church excludes anyone from its fellowship the basic humanity of those excluded is diminished, the church itself is diminished by restricting the redemptive work of God, and the humanity of those who do the excluding is diminished (Reynolds, 2008, p. 14). Failure to reach out to persons with disabilities not only furthers their isolation and alienation, but also separates and isolates the non disabled, limiting their own development and perspective on humanity by not being exposed to the full range of human ability. We must be clear on what it means to be human from a biblical perspective and acknowledge that every human being is created in God's image, irrespective of ability or achievement. Each human being is an individual, uniquely designed, gifted, and purposed (see chapter three and the exploration of several biblical themes).

We can add to what Reynolds said that excluding a person who is disabled from the opportunity to hear the gospel of Jesus Christ—whether out of ignorance and oversight or intentionally, assuming that the individual is neither worthy nor capable of receiving God's love—dishonors God, whose love and compassion are not limited. As we have already seen, Jesus's command is to take the good news to all peoples of the world, not just those society or culture says are deserving of God's grace. God's grace is *grace* because *no one* is deserving of it.

From my reading of Scripture, ministry to and with persons with disabilities is something which is close to the heart of God. The Christian Church should be a model for the rest of the world of inclusiveness and accessibility; a place where acceptance and welcome to all people is evident, and where grace is preached and practiced without reservation. Failure to demonstrate God's love for all humanity through action and words may result in the Church being associated with injustice and persecution of persons with disabilities.

We have already addressed the human tendency to sort people into categories of our own making, usually in a way in which "our" group comes out on top. Segregating people into groups reflects arrogance and pride, and in relation to disability, is often based on fear, ignorance, incorrect religious ideas, or superstition. Many able-bodied people view the birth to a child with a disability, or becoming disabled through some life event, as a tragedy because they imagine how this would impact their own life. Reinders (2011), however, asserted that many people with disabilities do not see their limitation as tragic:

Even in the case of acquired brain damage, the notion of tragedy does not offer a full, let alone a final description of people's lives. People with disabilities look at themselves as living a life with both potentialities and limitation, more or less like other people. (p. 60)

This somewhat optimistic outlook of disabled persons on life's possibilities may be diminished, however, by the negativity of temporarily able-bodied people. The man in John 5 *may* have had a more positive attitude in the early years of his life as a man with a disability, but after 38 years, his future seemed bleak to him, especially since he had no one to assist him. Any helpers he may have had from family or friends at the beginning perhaps grew weary of his dependence on them and cut off their relationship—particularly if they wrongly attributed his disability to personal sin.

Sometimes, separating ourselves from people with disabilities is because of insensitivity or ignorance about disability and the functional limitation it causes. This can lead people to feel overwhelmed by the person's situation and what they perceive to be his or her needs, but not knowing what to do. Some may believe meeting the needs of persons with disabilities is the responsibility of governmental or humanitarian organizations, allowing them to disavow any connectedness or responsibility toward disabled individuals or their families. But "humanitarianism" implies concern for and promotion of human welfare. Luke 4:18–19, Jesus's own description of his mission, clearly reveals his interest was in the *whole person*, not just the soul. Since Jesus's focus was humanitarian, this must also be the concern of the Christian Church.

The Church must seek to develop in its constituents, and model for the community, an inclusive worldview in which individuals with disabilities are recognized as having equal value as bearers of God's image. Ministry must be holistic, seeking to help disabled individuals develop physically, socially, behaviorally, spiritually, and relationally. Community-building and reconciliation should be primary objectives of the Christian Church—reconciliation first with God, but also with one another. The Church should give evidence of people living in a community of love and interdependence. As part of that community-building, however, it is imperative that the Church not see its role as only ministering *to* people with disabilities through evangelism and social outreach. Rather, persons with disabilities must be seen as important parts of the body of Christ, and welcomed into all aspects of kingdom life. Most certainly there is the goal of proclaiming Christ to persons with disabilities—they are as much in need of a Savior as able-bodied persons. But merely reaching out to include *"them,"* is insufficient. A fly caught in a spider web is "included" but still victimized (McCollum, 1998). We must seek to fully incorporate persons with disabilities into the life and fellowship of the church. This includes recognizing the gift they can be to us by their presence and love, and acknowledging that they also have spiritual gifts to be nurtured and providing opportunities for them to exercise these gifts within the Body of Christ—even allowing them to lead and teach the temporarily able-bodied as God enables and gifts them. People with disabilities must be seen as essential to the wholeness of the Christian community (Assemblies of God, 2000).

Recapping Some Biblical and Theological Principles

Let me briefly review some of what was discussed earlier as a way of guiding your thinking about doing ministry to and with persons with disabilities. Consider the following points, looking carefully at each Scripture cited, and taking note what is taught to consider its application in your life and ministry.

- ***Disabled persons are made in the image of God.*** They are no less marred by sin, and no less capable of restoration than those without disabilities. The Bible does not exempt persons with disabilities from its assertion that *all* have sinned and are in need of a Savior (Romans 3:23–24). The result of sin is death, spiritual and eternal, but the gift of God is eternal *life* (Romans 6:23). There is no justification for the failure of the Church to share the gospel of God's love with persons who are disabled.

- ***Jesus commanded that the gospel be preached to all people.*** God does not regard any people group as excluded from the scope of our evangelistic outreach (Mark 16:15). Jesus's promise of "abundant life" (John 10:10b) is not restricted to able-bodied believers alone. Sharing the gospel involves both evangelism and teaching with the goal of making disciples.

- ***The Church, as the people of God, is called to reach out to the neglected—the poor, the needy, the destitute, the hurting.*** Like the prophets of the Old Testament, we are to call for justice on behalf of the weak and oppressed. The Church is to be the voice of those who have no voice—both by challenging other Christians with the need to bring God's love to all people, and by challenging society and culture with the truth of God's Word (Exodus 23:6; Psalm 35:10, 140:12; Luke 14:15–24).

- ***The biblical mandate is that we not prefer one person over another.*** All human beings have the same standing before God, and have equal value as persons made in the image of God. In Philippians 2:3–4 Paul explained the attitude which we are to demonstrate (see also Romans 12:10). James 2:3–4 can be paraphrased to show its application to disability: "if you pay attention to the able-bodied person and say, 'You sit here in a good place,' while you say to the one who is disabled, 'You sit over there,' have you not then made distinctions among yourselves and become judges with evil thoughts?" How would such an attitude compare to the manner in which Jesus interacted with people who were disabled?

- ***We are commanded to love and to show kindness to others.*** Love for God and for others is the primary characteristic that should be evident in the life of believers (John 13:34). Christians are to be vessels through which God's love, mercy, and grace are shown to the world, consistently and intentionally, without regard for how the recipients of that love respond (Romans 13:8; Galatians 5:14). King David's treatment of Jonathan's son, Mephibosheth, who was physically disabled, is an example of this love in action (2 Samuel 9:1–3; see also 1 Samuel 20:14–17 as background).

Some have expressed concern over whether a person with a severe disability is cognitively able to understand the message of the gospel. We need to remember that the response of someone is not made by or dependent upon the evangelist, but by the individual as God's Spirit works in his or her heart. God's salvation is by his grace alone, not according to our ability to do something, or even to understand fully what God has done. Jesus once told his disciples that is was easier for a camel to pass through the eye of a needle than for a wealthy person to enter the kingdom of God. The disciples responded in amazement, "Who then can be saved?" Jesus answered, "with man this is impossible, but with God all things are possible" (Matthew 19:25–26). That same principle applies to individuals who are unable to respond verbally because of disability—what we may think impossible presents no challenge to God. We must not make the mistake of equating knowledge *about* Jesus with *knowing* Jesus as Lord. Carder (1984) related a comment made by a person with a cognitive disability: "I know I learn more slowly, but *my soul is not retarded"* (p. 153, emphasis added). We are not to judge who is or is not able to receive the gift of faith. Our responsibility is to be faithful in making the gospel visible through our words and actions. It is through God's grace we are saved, not through any works—or reasoning—of our own (Ephesians 2:8–10). Grace is not restricted by disability, even the most severe disability.

Practical Theology

Theology is usually thought to belong to the realm of those formally trained at seminary or Bible school. For many, the word "theology" conjures up volumes of systematically arranged thought about the Bible's teaching regarding such things as the Trinity, sin and salvation, the Church, and eschatology (end-times). For people without seminary training—and even for many who have—theology is a scholarly discipline, separate from daily life. But because God is living, our theology must also *live*. It must be relatable to life, especially when significant life changes occur. People have an innate need to make sense of their experience in order to feel some degree of control in their lives. Since God is a God of order not chaos, our need to bring meaning to our experience stems from our being created in God's image. Meaning-seeking can be particularly troublesome when personally encountering disability, such as becoming disabled or giving birth to a child with a disability. These events raise questions about what God is doing in our lives, or about punishment, or even whether God has abandoned us.

Theological study involves an ongoing search for the fullness of the truth of God (Migliore, 2004). Our readiness to seek meaning and to ask deep, sometimes troubling questions, is what makes theology *practical* and applicable in daily life. Theology is relevant in our analysis and interpretation of disability from a biblical perspective. We seek to reflect on what God is teaching through disability and our interactions with persons who are disabled—teaching about himself, ourselves, relationships and community, and Christian responsibility.

Rather than arising from or centering on academic reflection on Scripture, practical theology is context-related, beginning with our present life-experience. It is theology in action: We read Scripture in the context of ministry (for our purposes, ministry to and with persons affected by disability). Our goal is to understand the implications of Christian thought as a frame of reference for theologically interpreting our experiences and activities in the light of God's revelation of himself and his purposes in Scripture. This focus on understanding the implications of faith in guiding our actions is what makes practical theology *practical*. The question is not simply "What is going on?" when we encounter disability, but "What *should* be going on?" "How are we to live?" "How should I respond to what is happening?" "Where is God in this?" These intensely practical questions call for theological reflection on situations faced by individuals and families when disability enters their lives—as well as theological reflection about the community's and culture's interpretation of disability. Practical theological inquiry opens us "to the forming and transforming Spirit of God who remakes us as the image of Christ" (Osmer, 2008, p. 34). Thus, practical theology and spiritual formation are related.

Swinton (2000) claimed that "actions are themselves theological and as such are open to theological reflection" (p. 11). This implies that we should be concerned with what our actions "speak" to others about our theology and the trueness of our Christian witness. Do we show compassion and hospitality? Do our actions show a concern for biblical justice? Do we demonstrate Christlike character?

Jesus was himself a practical theologian. His *ministry* was as authoritative and revealing of God as his *teaching*. Jesus was not "a" word from God, but *the* Word of God (John 1:1, 14), a living embodiment of God's Word. His *life* was the message, and demonstrated his theology of God and humankind. Ordinary life situations and experiences provided context for his preaching and teaching. His preaching and teaching stressed the application of theology to specific incidences of the human experience. Often using parables, he explained and showed the spiritual significance of events, in the process correcting faulty interpretations and theology.

Our lives must evidence the same attitudes, actions, character, and manner of Jesus. As the Body of Christ, we must engage in theological reflection on life situations—our own and the life situation of others. As Jesus's representatives in the world today, we must *demonstrate* practical discipleship, not simply talk about being a disciple. It is in that practical discipleship that theological reflection leads to theological understanding:

> Understanding of God and the world comes about and is altered in a life of service to those who are the least of Christ's brothers and sisters. It means interpreting everyday life by means of the Bible rather than the study of the Bible being an end in itself cut off from involvement in everyday living. (Rowland & Bennet, 2006, p. 9)

Left Behind—on Purpose, for a Purpose

Some people argue that the Gospel message is simply a call to repentance and belief in the Lord Jesus Christ. But to limit our understanding of the Gospel to this presents an abbreviated Gospel. A more complete understanding of the good news of the Gospel starts by acknowledging that Jesus is the Messianic King, the promised Son of God, who came in human form as a servant (Romans 1:3–4; Philippians 2:4–9) and who, by his death and resurrection, brought atonement for our sin and secured our justification (Romans 3:34, 5:1, 9–11). Paul explained that Jesus's death on the cross released us from the dominion of sin and evil (Colossians 2:13–15). When Christ returns he will finalize what he began, completely renewing creation and resurrecting our bodies (Romans 8:19–26). In other words, the whole message of the Gospel includes what has yet to be done at the return of Christ. This eschatological element, largely not included in people's immediate thinking about the Gospel, has implications for ministry. Keller (2008) commented:

Texts like Luke 4:18 and Luke 6:20–35 show the implication of the gospel that the broken-hearted, unrecognized, and oppressed now have a central place in the economy of the Christian community, while the powerful and successful are humbled. Paul tells Peter that attitudes of racial and cultural superiority are "not in line" with the gospel of peace (Galatians 2:14). Generosity to the poor will flow from those who are holding fast to the gospel as their profession (2 Corinthians 9:13).

The recognition that Jesus will someday destroy hunger, disease, poverty, injustice, and death itself, should spur Christians to action and compassion when faced with these situations. Our desire should be to seek an end to situations that Jesus wants put right. When the disciples asked Jesus why a man was born blind, he explained that it was "that the works of God might be displayed in him" (John 9:3). The work to which Jesus referred was the man's being cured of his disability and, more importantly, his being healed spiritually (see John 9:35–38). But notice that in Jesus's answer to the disciples was an invitation to join with him in his ministry: "_We_ must work the works of him who sent me while it is day" (emphasis added). The work Jesus was sent to do included his atoning sacrifice, but also included the social aspects of his ministry that were in accord with his "mission statement" (Luke 4:18–20). Jesus intended that we, his disciples today, join with him in continuing that mission, bolstered by the knowledge that Jesus has paid the price of our acceptance and freedom and has given us the Holy Spirit to guide and inform us in our ministry.

That Jesus called us to be his disciples _here and now_, not when we get to heaven, has significant implications for our lives. Through Jesus's teaching and the example of his life we learn how we are to live. Jesus was the ultimate change agent, breaking down barriers between genders, ethnicities, social status, and disability/ability. Stearns (2010) explained that "being a Christian . . . requires much more than just having a _personal_ and transforming relationship with God. It also entails a _public_ and transforming relationship with the world" (p. 2, emphasis in original). The point is that believers have not just been saved _from_ something, in which case God could have simply taken us to be with him at the moment of conversion; God also saved us _for_ something. He has graced believers with salvation from sin's penalty but, since he has left us here, we understand that he has a purpose for each of us. Believers are commissioned to continue Jesus's mission of restoration and reconciliation as he explained it in the synagogue of Nazareth. Wright suggested that Christians are "to borrow from God's future in order to change the way things are in the present, to enjoy the taste of our eventual deliverance from evil by learning how to loose the bonds of evil in the present" (Wright, 2006, p. 147). In this way, Christians play a part in God's victory over evil:

> The new life of the Spirit, to which Christians are called in the present age, is not a matter of sitting back and enjoying spiritual comforts in a private, relaxed, easy-going spirituality, but consists rather of the unending struggle in the ministry of prayer, the struggle to bring God's wise, healing order into the world now, in implementation of the victory of the cross and anticipation of the final redemption. (Wright, 2006, p. 119).

Christian Social Ministry

The work of the Church is to take the Gospel and make disciples but, as shown above, this is not simply to spread the word. As with Jesus's earthly ministry, an essential part of the task is responding to and seeking to alleviate the cause and result of evil in the world. Watkins (1994) explained that Christian social ministry includes a call by God both to proclaim the good news through our verbal testimony and to demonstrate Christ's concern for the spiritual, physical, emotional, mental, and relational well-being of persons, families, and groups—both inside and outside the community of faith. Watkins noted that the Bible actually speaks more about ministry to persons who have social needs (such as those which flow from disability, disease, poverty, and oppression) than it does about verbal evangelism. Both evangelism and social ministry are to have a prominent place in the church's outreach. Watkins identified several principles for social ministry: it is rooted and grounded in God's love for all people; it recognizes and supports the worth, dignity, and integrity of each individual; it offers the kind of help a person can use to improve his or her own situation; and it shows concern for the whole person (1994, pp. 92–96). We can say that the essence of the church's social ministry is the great commandment as summarized and endorsed by Jesus: "'Love the Lord your God with all your heart, all your soul, and all your mind.' This is the first and most important command. And the second command is like the first: 'Love your neighbor as you love yourself'" (Matthew 22:37–40; cf. Deuteronomy 6:5 and Leviticus 19:18, especially in relation to Micah 6:8).

Social ministry such as working with persons affected by disability is, along with evangelism, part of the mission which Jesus gave to all his disciples (Matthew 28:18–20), a mission to bring healing and proclaim the kingdom. Ministry to the social needs of people, done in the name of Jesus Christ and motivated by love, is as much an evangelical task as our verbal witness. That this continues to be our Christian responsibility is evident in the fact that Jesus did not simply take us to be with him and the time of our salvation. As I said earlier, we have been left behind on purpose and for a purpose. We remain, not just to verbally share the good news of salvation with others, but to demonstrate the reality of the good news through our interaction with people unlike ourselves and doing all that God enables us to do to bring social change for those oppressed and rejected by the powerful majority—as a foretaste of what things will be like when the final part of God's story (consummation) is accomplished.

Church-Based Ministry

We can describe the role of the Church as fourfold: redemptive, reconciliative, rehabilitative, and reciprocal. The **redemptive role** is patterned after that of Jesus. In his earthly ministry, Jesus reached out to the unrighteous, poor, captives, blind, downtrodden, crippled, lame—to the whole world—with the gift of salvation. In similar fashion, the Church, as the Body of Christ operative in the world today, is to carry on that ministry by bringing the good news of salvation through Christ to all peoples.

The **reconciliative role** highlights the reconciliation with God that Jesus has brought about (Romans 5:11; 2 Corinthians 5:18). But as we have already seen, the reconciliation Jesus accomplished also involved breaking down walls which have separated people (cf. Galatians

3:28; Colossians 3:11). Paul specifically says in Romans 10:12 that there is no difference between Jew and Gentile. The principle behind Paul's words can easily be extended to say that in God's eyes there is no difference between the disabled and the temporarily able-bodied. Acts 10:34 and Romans 2:11 clearly teach that God does not show favoritism or partiality. Just as clearly taught is the principle that believers should not show favoritism (James 2:1, 9), but that we are to be devoted to one another and to honor others (Romans 12:10, 16; Philippians 2:3–4). Beyond reconciliation with God and with one another, our ministry to and with persons who are disabled must address reconciliation of disabled persons with themselves; that is, helping them to realize they are valued and loved by God, and to learn that despite their "weakness"—or even *through* their weakness—they can still serve and glorify God. Better to have a "weak" body, but have God in your heart, than to be strong, but to enter eternity without Christ. This type of reconciliation involves "owning" one's disability, that is, acknowledging it as a part of who they are, and including it as part of their "story," choosing to go on with the disability, instead of going on as if it were not a part of who they are, or refusing to go on at all (Langer, 2011). Both those who are not disabled and those who are must learn that they are—and have—much more than the disability.

The **rehabilitative role** builds on the redemptive and reconciliative roles in that it focuses on social and spiritual "rehabilitation" for those who have become disabled. This centers partly on the responsibility to go beyond mere evangelism to discipleship. It involves helping others to grow in their relationship with God and their understanding of his Word. For persons who have become disabled through accident or illness, it means helping them to accept their "new" body and to rebuild skills or learn compensatory skills for living. Spiritual rehabilitation for such persons is related to their becoming reconciled with themselves and with God, who remains sovereign and compassionate despite the disability, and whose presence is assured even in the midst of physical and spiritual pain and confusion (cf. 2 Corinthians 12:7–10; Hebrews 13:5).

Finally, the **reciprocal role** takes one further step in recognizing interdependence and community. It acknowledges our need for one another, and affirms that both the temporarily able-bodied and those with disabilities can minister to and alongside one another. It appreciates the fact that all believers have at least one spiritual gift which God intends for us to use in building up his Church, and that having a disability neither prohibits persons from participating in ministry nor limits them to being only recipients of ministry from others. "Weak and seemingly inferior people may seem to lack importance, but placed in the hands of the Master they can be a masterpiece" (Tada & Jensen, 1997, p. 32).

Ultimately, the goal of disability ministry is the same as for any other form of ministry: to glorify God through the proclamation of the Gospel and through living a life that brings honor to the One who has called us to be his children. But more specifically, disability ministry seeks to:

- Open doors to sharing the Gospel with disabled persons

- Integrate people with disabilities into the life of the church

- Model inclusivity and fellowship to the greater community and to the culture

- Demonstrate the love of Christ in action

- Meet the spiritual, physical, relational, and emotional needs of persons with disabilities and their families

The desire is to create a welcoming faith community into which persons with disabilities can be readily integrated, not simply as part of the congregation, but as an intimate part of the local body of Christ. God's intent is that his house be a house of prayer for *all* people (Isaiah 56:7, emphasis added). This will require taking steps to eliminate architectural or communication, attitudinal or theological, and aspirational barriers which would prevent persons with disabilities from participating and feeling welcomed and valued in the fellowship.

Involving the Whole Church in Disability Ministry

When seeking to involve church members in disability ministry, some might argue that this is not their "job." Such a statement implies a negative view of disability and people with disabilities, and a disavowal of any responsibility to their neighbor, at least neighbors who are judged to be of lesser or no worth. I suggest, however, that such ministry is not a *job*. It is part of our calling to be like Jesus, and part of our commission to bring the Gospel to all peoples. God can use this ministry to help us be conformed to the image of Christ. Rather than being a job, ministry to and with people with disabilities is a *privilege*. Platt asserted,

> Anyone wanting to proclaim the glory of Christ to the ends of the earth must consider not only how to declare the gospel verbally but also how to demonstrate the gospel visibly in a world where so many are urgently hungry [for good news]. (2010, p. 109)

It is a serious matter to God how we, as his representatives, respond to people with disabilities, the poor, and the powerless.

It is essential that the senior pastor be enthusiastic in his or her support of disability ministry, and models for the congregation acceptance of persons who are disabled. But the senior pastor is not necessarily the person who will (or must) be solely responsible. The faithfulness and effectiveness of each individual church is not measured by what the pastor does, but by the action and attitude of all who are a part of the church (Stearns, 2010). Most pastors are already deeply involved in ministry activity; to expect them also to be the main person to carry out disability ministry could place them in a position leading to spiritual or physical "burnout." We must also be respectful of the pastor's family and not add another burden that could disrupt family relationships. Nonetheless, the pastor and church leaders play a crucial role in sensitizing the congregation to the importance of disability ministry and to the opportunity to become involved in practical Christianity and potentially impact the culture with the Gospel. Once the pastor has a clear understanding of the need for outreach and ministry to individuals and families affected by disability, his or her role as an equipper of the congregation will involve communicating the vision for disability ministry, committing the need to the Lord in persistent prayer, and waiting expectantly for God to raise up others to come alongside or to take the lead in such ministry.

To be effective in this role requires that pastors as well as other leaders in the church critically examine their personal attitude toward persons with disabilities. It is imperative that Scripture be studied to understand God's view of persons with disabilities and to learn basic truths about the causes of disability in order to dispel misconceptions and theological errors about disability and people who have disabilities. At the same time, the pastor and others involved in the ministry must become informed about the individuals in the local community who are disabled. Sometimes a church leader will say that they have no people with disabilities in their church or community and question the need for engaging in disability ministry. But many persons with disabilities are kept out of sight as long as possible because of fear that the entire family may be rejected. It is not uncommon for church and community leaders to be unaware of the existence of persons with disabilities in their village or community. One village chief in Cameroon insisted, with much self-assurance, that there were no people with disabilities in his "realm." But when he responded to an invitation to come to the town hall to observe an evangelistic outreach to disabled individuals from his village, he found 95 persons, mostly adults, who had hearing, visual, or cognitive impairments in attendance!

Evangelism of Persons with Disabilities

The necessity of doing evangelism with persons who have disabilities is the same as for everyone else: all have sinned and are under the sentence of death (Romans 3:23, 6:23), and Jesus is the only way of salvation (John 14:6; Acts 4:12). We are to follow Jesus's example of incarnational ministry (John 1:14), freely and openly relating to persons with disabilities in love and humble service (John 13:5–14) and with the same attitude as Christ displayed (Philippians 2:5–11). Our presence and willingness to become involved with people who have disabilities is a witness to the change that Jesus has wrought in our own lives. But more than that, building a relationship with persons who are disabled opens the way for us to give verbal testimony to who Jesus is, and what reconciliation with God through Jesus's sacrifice on the cross and subsequent resurrection can mean for them.

However, many people who are disabled will be hesitant or resistant if someone unknown approaches them in a public setting. Their experience of rejection, abuse, or exploitation at the hands of the able-bodied, sometimes even within their own family, leads to suspicion of other's motives. Consequently, building a trusting relationship with persons who are disabled is essential, but may take time (just as it may between persons who are able-bodied). Patience and consistency in extending the love of Jesus to people with disabilities is necessary. Recipients of this outreach need to learn that your motivation is pure; that you are not seeking to take advantage of someone who, because of disability, may be vulnerable.

Some special considerations in doing evangelism with persons who are disabled need to be noted. It is essential to remember that we are dealing with *persons* of inherent value; they are not "projects" or "prospects," which would imply that our interest is simply to add another convert to our credit (which, if this is our motivation, certainly belies the principle of love and humility mentioned above). Rather, we must remember that each one with whom we seek to share the gospel is a *person*, a unique individual. We must get to know the person, and treat the individual with the same respect we would like others to show us. The Church is to be characterized by hospitality (Romans 12:12; Hebrews 13:2; 1 Peter 4:9), which begins by recognizing our commonalities rather than our differences. (Recall what was said in chapter one about their being more similarities than differences between disabled and with able-bodied persons.) It is important to learn as much as possible about the individual and develop a friendship between the person and yourself. It is helpful to learn something about disabilities in general so that our approach and ministry can be adjusted as necessary, but we must also remember that two individuals with the same disabling conditions may vary greatly in their needs and abilities. We must speak directly *to* and *with* the individual who has the disability, not "through" a family member or personal caregiver. For comfort sake and to communicate respect, speak with the person who has the disability at eye-level (for instance, if the person is seated in a wheelchair). Be encouraging and flexible; model patience and comfort in interacting with the person, and seek to establish a good, trusting relationship.

Suggestions for Outreach

Exactly how your church's disability ministry will be structured will depend on your present church facility and programs and the availability of willing workers to carry on this ministry. But at the very least, your ministry must make clear that people with disabilities are welcome into the worship experience at your church. They must know they are welcome, they must be addressed cordially, and appropriate accommodations must be made for them to be able to participate in the worship experience. Opportunities must be afforded for persons with disabilities to engage in the same types of activity that are available to the non disabled—worship, Sunday School, Bible study, and other aspects of fellowship designed to strengthen and develop the Body of Christ. Churches could also explore the possibilities of developing mentoring programs or "friendship groups" that can meet spiritual and relational needs and help in the reconciliative and rehabilitative roles of the church. If necessary and available, assistance with transportation (by personal auto, taxi, or simply a volunteer wheelchair-pusher) can help communicate to disabled persons that they are valued and welcomed. And we must not forget that the family members—parents, siblings, and extended family—are also affected by the presence of a disabled family member and need to be graced with the love, compassion, and hospitality of the church.

Some churches have established *Barnabas Ministries* with the goal of bringing encouragement to others by word and action. Service groups from the church can assist families with normal tasks such as shopping or laundering; provide respite care to allow parents or families to have a break from caregiving; tutor children who are not able to go to school or need extra help in learning; or mentoring adults who have become disabled so they can learn a new trade. Or they can simply spend time in fellowship with the family or individual. Christians who engage in these kinds of activities need basic information about the specific disability and what specific needs the individual has (such as proper seating and positioning of a person who has a physical disability). The most essential necessity is a loving heart and a desire to be the hands and feet of Jesus to the families involved.

Several special programs to promote disability awareness and ministry have been suggested by the Joni and Friends International Disability Center[5] which may be used effectively in many cultures, with appropriate adaptation as necessary. Consider these ideas and modify them as needed for your cultural situation.

- *Disability Awareness Sunday:* Focusing on the need of the congregation to learn about people with disabilities from God's perspective

- *Disability Outreach Sunday:* Direct outreach to people with disabilities in the community

- *"Barrier-Free" Sunday:* Focusing on the need to break down architectural and attitudinal barriers that separate people

- *Access to God Sunday:* Emphasizing the need for *all* people to access God's blessing and fellowship with other believers

- *Power in Weakness Sunday:* Showing how God's power is manifested through weakness

- *Jars of Clay Sunday:* Recognizing that we are all earthen vessels (2 Corinthians 4:7) to transport God's mercy, and that people with disabilities are part of the church as equal vessels

- *Luke 14 Sunday:* Illustrating the need to invite people with disabilities to fill God's house by teaching from Luke 14 about the "great banquet"

- *Disability Ministry Sunday:* Highlighting the ministry of the church with all God's people

- *Through the Roof Sunday:* Using the story from Mark 2 of the four friends who brought a paralyzed man to Jesus by lowering him through the roof as an example of ministry

- *Disability Friendship Sunday*: Stressing communion and oneness of all believers, including those with disabilities

Many of the above can be a focus of the sermon (there are many passages in Scripture that are applicable to issues of disability). But whenever possible, the message will be more effective if persons with disabilities can be involved in the presentation in some way. When serving as a missionary-teacher in Cameroon, I worked in association with an indigenous ministry, the Center for Empowerment of Females with Disabilities (CEFED). CEFED held evangelistic meetings focusing on people with disabilities in various villages. Those who came to the outreach received the Gospel message and a Bible (cleansing and feeding for the soul), and were given gifts: soap (cleansing for the body) and rice (feeding the body). We held special services in churches designed to make the congregations aware of the need and the opportunity to minister to disabled individuals, and help them see the *abilities* of people with disabilities. The Director

---

[5] Joni and Friends International Disability Center is headquartered in Agoura Hills, California. JAF has several programs including *Wheels for the World*, which collects, repairs, and distributes refurbished wheelchairs to persons with disabilities in many countries throughout the world; *Family Retreats* for families with a disabled member; *Total Access* programs which help churches and families make buildings architecturally accessible; and disability awareness training for churches and seminaries. Visit JAF Ministries' website at http://www.joniandfriends.org/

of CEFED, herself physically disabled, gave her testimony; disabled children from the CEFED Special School served as a worship team to lead the congregation in praise songs; one of the children read the Scripture passage; a man who was physically disabled led the church in prayer; and a message was given based on the parable of the great banquet (Luke 14:12–24).

Involving Persons with Disabilities in the Church

It is important that believers who are disabled are given opportunity to be involved in worship and service opportunities in the church. We must not assume that because a person has a disability he or she has nothing to offer—to God, by way of service, or to us personally, in the way of friendship. And temporarily able-bodied persons must not assume that they are always the better or stronger person in the sense of ability, knowledge, or spirituality. Care must be taken not to define persons with disabilities by their needs, but to be open to receive the gift which they can be to all of us.

We have already noted that God has designed every individual, able-bodied or disabled, with certain abilities and interests, and has given at least one Spiritual gift to every believer. He expects those gifts and abilities to be used wisely and responsibly in service to him and to others. The church must not prevent any believer, disabled or temporarily able-bodied, from serving the Lord and his people. Wheelchair users and persons with other disabling conditions may be just as able as non disabled persons to share musically, lead in prayer, read God's Word in the worship service, serve as a greeter or usher, lead a Bible study class, or preach.

Persons with disabilities should also be included in Christian education programs such as Sunday School, youth group, and adult Bible study, as participants or, if qualified, as leaders. Hoeksema (1990) pointed out that people who have disabilities have many of the same gifts as able-bodied persons, and should be able to use those gifts in worship. Not being able to read print does not mean a person cannot read a Braille Bible. Using crutches or a wheelchair does not prevent a person from gracing others with their singing ability. Being cognitively impaired neither lessens nor negates the genuineness of a person's public profession of faith in Christ. You may be surprised to find that persons with a disability contribute more to the fellowship of believers than they receive!

Amegatcher (2011) stated that the presence in the church of sick, poor, and disabled persons is an important reminder of the ministry of Jesus as shown by the Gospel writers. She cautioned against making the church a "museum of 'bright, shiny' people or 'catalogue model teenagers'" and still consider ourselves part of the same ministry as Jesus (p. 289). She pointed to the important witness that is presented to the world when Christians embrace and include the same kinds of people that Jesus embraced and included.

Going Deeper

1. Revisit your responses to "Going Deeper" at the end of chapter three. Identify the barriers that exist in your church (and community) and determine how those barriers can be eliminated. What resources, programs, teaching, or supports are needed to enable people with disabilities to be included in your church fellowship?

2. How do you respond to this statement: "Ministry is spirit to spirit. It does not depend on the state of a person's eyesight, hearing, ability to walk, talk, or sit still. Nor does it depend on one's intellect. It depends on one's heart" (Sieck & Hartvigsen, 2001, p. iii).

3. Joel 2:32, Acts 2:21, Romans 10:13 all state that "whoever calls upon the name of the Lord will be saved." Does this necessarily require an audible "call"?

4. Several goals for disability ministry were presented in the chapter. What additional goals can you propose for disability ministry in your church community?

5. What ways can you identify that would be appropriate in your community/culture to reach out to people with disabilities in the community?

6. To help in planning ministry to and with persons with disabilities, consider the following questions:

    a. How can you (or your church) broaden and deepen people's circle of friends so that they include persons with disabilities?

    b. What role can you (or your church) play in increasing the presence and welcoming of disabled people in the community and in the church?

    c. How can you (or your church) assist people who are disabled to develop personal competencies and skills and to become involved in the body life of your church?

    d. How can you (or your church) disciple persons with disabilities so that they grow in Christ and discover, develop, and use their gifts in service to Christ and others?

Chapter Six

Ministering to Families Affected by Disability

It must be remembered that the presence of a person with a disability in a family means the *entire family* has special physical, material, and spiritual needs. Stigma attached to disability (and, thus, to the individual who is disabled), can easily spread to the entire family resulting in isolation. Isolation can also be self-imposed, because of fear of people's reaction or shame imposed by the culture's view of disability. Family members need to understand that being disabled does not mean a person has no value, is cursed, brings a curse on the family, or any of the other degrading ways disability and disabled persons have been viewed. Hence, the *family* is in as much need of compassionate outreach and ministry as the individual who is disabled.

Impact of Disability on the Family

Disability can significantly impact family dynamics, disrupting the typical or expected manner in which family members relate. In some cultures, disabilities resulting from genetic or birth complications lead a father to blame and reject both the mother and the child, or to openly deny being the father of the child. It is not uncommon for a father to reject both his wife and the child because of his inability to accept the situation, particularly if the first-born male child is disabled. Frequently, the child born with an obvious disability, if not intentionally left to die, is kept hidden from the community as long as possible. Regardless of the gender of the child, dreams of what the child would be like and would contribute to the family or community are shattered once the disability is evident.

Because many associate disability with sin, judgment, or being "cursed," becoming disabled changes how family members view the individual, particularly if the person's disability is believed to prevent her or him from contributing to the welfare of the family or society in general. That assumption may lead parents to forego securing education for a disabled child or from seeking assistance from medical or governmental organizations that could offer help. In some countries, doctors may assume it is not worth the effort to treat a sick child who is disabled, or that a disabled adult will not be able to pay for services, and choose to help able-bodied patients only. Even in more developed nations, some physicians may provide only limited service to persons with disabilities or argue against taking "heroic measures" to treat someone with a severe disability. Many physicians assume a disability will result in a poor *quality of life*—a judgment which no one can make with accuracy, and a situation which is more dependent on how society views and treats the individual than on the disabling condition itself. Often, little thought is given to the *sanctity of life*—the recognition that life is a gift from God and that all are created in the image of God.

Family Stress

These negative thoughts and responses are attitudinal barriers that bring added stress on family members. The degree of stress experienced will depend on a number of personal, familial, social, and spiritual factors. ***Person-centered factors*** include such things as the nature and severity of the disability, its impact on the individual's functioning, the age of the person when becoming disabled, and the person's own self-concept. ***Family-centered factors*** include the family's understanding of the disabling condition, how the disability and the individual are perceived by family members, the strength or quality of relationships within the family, the size of the immediate family, the availability and attitude of the extended family, and the real or perceived special needs of the person who is disabled. ***Socially-centered factors*** include negative attitudes of the community toward the person (stigma, isolation, exclusion), the availability and accessibility of medical and other community services and supports, and concerns of the family related to education or vocation. ***Spiritually-related factors*** combine many of these ideas, but focus primarily on how the disability is understood and where God is in this experience, along with basic questions related to evil and suffering (chapter eight will discuss this issue).

Family Reactions

When a person gives birth to a child who is obviously disabled, or when an individual becomes disabled through illness, injury, or ageing, various reactions are often observed in the family or the affected individual. Initial reactions frequently include shock, denial, seeking someone to blame, and inappropriate and unproductive guilt. Other common reactions include depression and withdrawal, displaced anger, and bargaining with God ("if you remove the disability, I promise to be a good person"). Sometimes, the family or the individual who has become disabled will engage in doctor-shopping, hoping to find a doctor who can give a "better" prognosis. This often leads to increased debt or poverty on the part of the family, as unscrupulous doctors or "healers" take advantage of the situation, offering help in return for money when there is actually little or nothing they are able to do. Because their child may not reach typical developmental milestones (e.g., standing, walking, or talking) at the same time as non disabled children of the same age, the parents of a child who is disabled may have difficulty relating to other families. They must also deal with unfavorable reactions to their child by children who are temporarily able-bodied—even from other families and children within the church.

The family that is dealing with disability has become part of a unique cultural group, one which able-bodied individuals do not understand. The family is exposed to a new "language" of medical, psychological, and educational words, which doctors and teachers may or may not define or explain (in some cultures, to ask a doctor questions is regarded as offensive, even if only seeking clarity). The individuals and families affected by disability must establish a new "normal," since their experience will be different from that of people who are not dealing with issues of disability.

The desired reaction, one which reflects a more realistic and mature response, is acceptance of the person or the condition without any devaluation, and adjusting expectations accordingly but without settling for less than the person is capable of doing or becoming. This is also the reaction desired of non disabled persons upon meeting someone with a disability.

Several avenues for church ministry become evident as we consider the impact of disability on individuals and families. Churches can model and promote acceptance of the individual and the family; provide appropriate information about the disability to the family and the congregation; meet emotional and physical needs of the entire family; be "present" to the individual and family, showing compassion and hospitality as a representative of Christ; offer biblical counseling and instruction related to questions of God's love and sovereignty; and encourage hope and perseverance centered on a proper relationship with Christ. Simple acts which communicate respect and appreciation, demonstrate our availability, and promote relationships are essential to affirm the personhood and acceptance of the one who is disabled. These may also be things which the individual and the family affected by disability do not typically experience.

The "Wounds" of Disability

Wolf Wolfensberger, formerly a professor at Syracuse University, produced a body of work that continues to have a significant place in disability studies (cf. Gaventa & Coulter, 2001). Wolfensberger championed the idea of *normalization*, which helped fuel the movement toward inclusion of persons with disabilities in schools and society. He developed an approach known as *Social Role Valorization* (cf. Wolfensberger, 1972, 1983, 2000), which seeks to counter the negative valuation of persons with disabilities and promote a life-affirming approach to interacting with them. Wolfensberger spoke of "wounds" which people and families affected by disability often experience. The first two wounds he suggested are the bodily or intellectual impairment itself and the functional limitations which result—wounds which are, of course, situated within the individual who is disabled. The rest of the wounds Wolfensberger identified, however, are external to the person and are directly connected to the attitudes and response of people who are not disabled. These wounds can be grouped into four categories: those related to the person's social status and valuation by others; wounds of rejection and segregation; wounds dealing with personal relationships, freedom, and community; and material and experiential wounds. Evidence of these types of wounds can be seen in the life of the man Jesus encountered in John 5, as brought out in the following table.

Social "Wounds" of Disability Illustrated in the Experience of the Man in John 5:1-17

Wounds caused by attitudes of	Wounds in the life of the man in
Status Being assign to a lower social status; seen a "deviant"; labeling (stigmatizing); seen as the basis for their own problems or problems of others	Known only as the "invalid" (technically meaning no validity, or being irrelevant); cast in the role of a beggar; disability probably seen as a result of personal sin
Rejection Overt or covert rejection; being segregated from the community and grouped with others with disabilities; abandonment; seen as a burden on others or society itself	Loneliness, absence of anyone to help him; pushed aside by the civil and religious leaders; possibly abandoned by family to "live" by the pool; separation from healthy human relationships
Personal Absence or loss of genuine relationships; loss of autonomy and freedom; being thought less than human; exclusion from participation in higher-order value systems that would provide community	No family or friends to help; no independence; no freedom or opportunity to worship with the community, to be schooled, to learn a trade; seen only as "the disabled man"
Material/Experiential Separation from or lack of connection to the physical environment; physical and material poverty; exploitation.	Disconnected from the physical environment beyond the pool; absence of meaningful, caring relationship with others; limited personal possessions; no opportunity or encouragement to discover and use personal talents (and probably no expectation, on his part or from others, that he has an talent or ability)

Ministry with those dealing with disability begins with understanding our responsibility to be ministers of God's grace—to *re-present* his grace in the world. These wounds of disability become hindrances to the development of people with disabilities and their integration into society. They also impact the family. Most of these wounds are actually *spiritual* wounds (they affect the person's and family's spirit) needing pastoral (spiritual) care. People with disabilities are not simply a complex of impersonal problems to be solved (Reinders, 2008), but are people who share the human need to love and be loved.

Pastoral Care

The kingdom mandate for ministry shown in Jesus's parable of the sheep and the goats (Matthew 25:31–45) is to serve human needs without respect of persons. The clear implication of the parable is that *all* Jesus's disciples are to engage in such activities as providing food and nourishment to the hungry and thirsty, according hospitality to aliens, visiting the imprisoned, and caring for those who are physically diseased or disabled. By so responding to the needs of individual who fall into these categories, Christians identify with "the in-breaking of God's kingdom in the world and move with God in the realm of human affairs" (Sanders, 1997, p. 28).

Pastoral care has to do with the entire church community *acting out* the gospel and revealing a new way of being human, fundamental to which is caring for others (Swinton, 1999). Ministry to persons with disabilities is something that the whole Body of Christ must engage in. Christians must understand their role as ministers of God's grace and love in the world. Paul urged that believers not be conformed to the pattern of this world, but be transformed through the renewal of their minds—changing how they think in order to "test and approve" the purposes of God in and through their life (Romans 12:2). The result is a new way of *seeing* and *being* in God's world, "seeing the world through God's eyes," as Swinton said. This includes a change in how we see, value, and respond to persons who are disabled. All Christians need to regard people with disabilities with the same compassion and welcoming attitude that Jesus demonstrated.

Pastoral care is not something only the pastor of the church gives. It does not require a degree in counseling, or even formal theological training. Every Christian should be ready to provide pastoral care to others. The term refers to the idea of shepherding others—leading, guiding, supporting, counseling. It is akin to the term *spiritual direction,* which Simon Chan (1998) described as "a dynamic relationship that exists between two person as one helps the other grow in the Christian life" (p. 226).

To provide pastoral or spiritual care to families affected by disability requires several things. Some of the most important are a proper understanding of disability and God's view of disability and disabled persons; a commitment to hospitality, interdependence, and biblical justice; a humble, servant attitude, recognizing our role of re-presenting Christ to others; an ability to develop healthy, respectful, and non-judgmental relationships; an open communication style; and the ability to identify the needs of others. Essential to all of this is the ability to relate Scriptural and theological truths to the practical issues faced by those who are the recipients of pastoral care.

Pastoral care recognizes our responsibility as Christians to love one another as Jesus commanded (John 13:34–35; John 15:12, 17). To love as Jesus loved brings to the world a living example of God's love, and a witness to God's demonstration of that love on Calvary. The parable of the Good Samaritan (Luke 10:26–37) teaches that our neighbor is anyone we encounter who has a need. This love to our neighbor (whether that person is a fellow believer or not), consists of desiring the greater good of the person and the intention to do whatever we can to meet his or her needs. Paul's teaching about how we are to treat one another helps us understand how to pastorally care for others, including an untiring willingness to forgive and bear with others.[6]

Characteristics of Pastoral/Spiritual Caregiving

Pastoral, or spiritual care involves compassionate presence. This means we must be ready to build relationships with others and bathe that relationship in prayer, recognizing that each of us is dependent on God for wisdom and direction. Essential characteristics of caregiving are compassion, empathy, commitment to others, active listening, and remaining free from preconceived notions as to the needs and abilities of the person and family affected by disability (cf. Shelly, 2000). Undergirding all of these characteristics is an attitude of humility—consciously laying aside any thought that we are better than those we seek to minister with. Also significant is an attitude of vulnerability, a willingness to be open to the other. Vulnerability serves as a "catalyst which brings us into community" (Browne, 1997). Vulnerability acknowledges that we all have needs, and we are all susceptible to disability through accident, illness, or ageing. Jesus demonstrated these characteristics in his life and ministry, and Paul reinforced them in his directive in Romans 12:15–16.

God is a God of compassion and expects his children to be people of compassion, also. Our call is "to imitate Jesus in seeking restoration of broken relationships, becoming present to those in difficulty, delivering those in situations where God's compassion seems distant, and forgiving others in order to restore them to community" (Truex, 1992, p. 57). But compassion is not something "handed down" to those in need from a position of superiority. Humility and vulnerability flow from a position of equality. Just as Jesus took on human form to minister to humankind, we must be "incarnate" to those we provide pastoral/spiritual care.

Empathy helps to develop informed compassion. People with disabilities generally do not need or want pity; rather, they want to be understood and appreciated as fellow human beings. Empathy results from our willingness to identify with those we minister to, recognizing our common humanity and value as God's image-bearers. Empathy requires active listening to gain insight into the life experience of others. We must resist the human tendency to offer opinions or judgments without first truly hearing or understanding the person. We must encourage them to be as self-determining as possible, given the limitations of the disabling condition, acting on their own preferences rather than our presumptions.

Families and individuals who deal with disability often ask "Why?" We must not be too quick to answer the question (without the mind of God, how could we know the "why" of anything?). Again, the principle of humility demands that we not attempt to make pronouncements based on our often faulty thinking. It is the quality of care that we provide that is important, not our theories about what God may be taking the person through. We need to learn from God's disapproval of the wrong-headed counsel of Job's friends who offered counsel (really, more of

---

[6]   See, for example, Romans 12:10, 16 and 15:5,7; 1 Corinthians 12:25; 2 Corinthians 13:11; Galatians 6:2; Ephesians 4:2, 32; Colossians 3:13, 16; 1 Thessalonians 4:18 and 5:11, 15.

a judgment) without any understanding. Active, empathetic listening can help us to become aware of the person's or family's fears, thoughts, and needs so that we are able to respond more appropriately.

Each of these characteristics of pastoral/spiritual care, when honestly and consistently a part of our ministry, communicate to the individual or family acceptance, respect, and value. The disabling condition and the resulting needs are acknowledged, but so is the *person*. Our acceptance of the person who is disabled helps the person accept herself or himself as one who is created in God's image, and as an equal part of the faith community. Hopefully, establishing a warm relationship with the family or individual dealing with disability will enable both caregiver and the disabled person to identify characteristics of the individual or family which may be used in ministry to others (cf. Webb-Mitchell, 1988). Pastoral/spiritual care to people affected by disability can be patterned after the behavior of the "Good Samaritan" in Jesus's parable (Luke 10:25–37).

Lessons from Jesus's Example

Jesus's actions during his earthly ministry provide many examples for us to follow in providing pastoral/spiritual care to others. I will highlight just a few that illustrate important elements for disability ministry.

The Samaritan Woman

In John 4, we read of Jesus's meeting with a Samaritan woman. This is significant because in openly speaking with the woman, Jesus demonstrated his willingness to break through barriers, in this case gender and ethnic barriers, and to establish a relationship that resulted in spiritual change in the woman and in many from her village. His crossing these barriers was intentional—we are told that he *had* to pass through Samaria to reach Galilee (John 4:4). But his having to go through Samaria was not geographically required, in fact, most Jews would avoid passing through Samaria by crossing over the Jordan River and traveling north, even though this would lengthen their journey. Jesus's meeting with this woman was not an accident—it was a "divine appointment." Similarly, we must intentionally cross barriers of attitude, fear, or embarrassment in order to establish relationships with people and families dealing with disability.

Jesus began conversing with the woman by raising a physical need (his thirst), but quickly directed the conversation toward her spiritual needs, building a bridge from the physical (drawing water) to the spiritual (living water). Jesus, of course, knew her needs and her history, which would not be immediately true of us when beginning a relationship with someone who is disabled. But we must seek to determine those needs through observation and conversation. We must resist any assumption we have as to the person's or family's specific situational needs, since their experience is significantly different from ours. Instead, respectfully ask questions that are pertinent (not just out of curiosity), and honor what may be shared in confidence.

Nonetheless, in terms of spiritual needs, we are safe to assume that the person or family needs hope, love, and acceptance. They need to be assured that God created them in his image and loves them, even if disabled. They need to understand that God is not a vengeful God who is punishing them for something by "sending" disability. They need to know that Jesus died for them as well as for persons who are able-bodied. We must help them gain a positive outlook, which includes gaining a biblical understanding of suffering. Note that Jesus's "blessing" to the woman of Samaria spread to others from her village (John 4:39–42). Similarly, spiritual care directed toward the person who is disabled can spill over to the immediate and extended family—even, possibly, to the community.

The Man at the Pool

In chapter one we explored John 5, Jesus's meeting with the man who was disabled for 38 years. In this encounter, note how Jesus modeled respect as he approached the man. His question to the man—"Do you want to be made well?"—would seem to have an obvious answer: Our presumption would be that the man wanted this very much. But Jesus treated the man respectfully and sought to actively involve him in what was to happen. Jesus did the same with Bartimaeus, a blind beggar who cried out for mercy (Mark 10:46–52). Jesus asked Bartimaeus, "What do you want me to do for you?" Surely, with both men, Jesus knew the disability and their desire to be cured, but he respectfully engaged them. In a similar fashion, we need to resist acting on our assumptions. Our assumptions *may* be correct, but it is better to ask—just as we would rather be asked than have someone tell us what we need or want based on his or her perspective. A simple application of this principle is that if we are ministering to someone who is a wheelchair user, we must not simply grab the wheelchair and begin to push the individual, assuming that we know where he or she wishes to go. The wheelchair is like a part of the person's body; respect demands that we ask if they would like assistance as well as asking where they would like to go or be placed.

There is another significant point we learn from Jesus's encounter with the man by the pool that is a guide for our ministry to people with disabilities. Jesus's specific focus was on the man's physical need and the wounds created by his segregation from the community (having no one to assist him). Jesus did not directly address the man's spiritual need of a saving relationship with God, something which he rather quickly addressed with the Samaritan woman. It was not until later, when Jesus located the man in the Temple, that he raised a spiritual issue: "See, you are well! Sin no more, that nothing worse may happen to you" (John 5:14). Jesus was not saying the man's disability was a result of sin (which had no significance to Jesus in curing him). Rather, Jesus was warning him that to live a life of sin would lead to "something worse," that is, eternal damnation. To provide pastoral care to people and families affected by disability, we must lay aside any thought that unconfessed personal sin is the reason for the disability. We recognize the need for forgiveness and reconciliation with God, but it is important to first establish a relationship with those we seek to minister to. That may well include identifying some physical or material needs that we can meet. People who have lived with a disability for some time will tend to be skeptical, questioning the reason for our attention and the legitimacy of our motives. We need to be patient in building a relationship, doing what we can to show friendship and genuine concern before seeking a "decision for Christ." For example, if we present a wheelchair to someone who has a physical disability, and then ask if they would like to accept Christ into their life, it is unlikely that the person will say "no" out of fear that the wheelchair gift might be rescinded. Patience and an ongoing relationship is essential, just as it would be in any discipleship program.

The Need for Hope

Along with consistent love and respect, individuals and families dealing with disability need hope. In Lamentations 3, Jeremiah spoke about personal affliction, thereby identifying with the sufferings of the people of Judah. Although the name of God is not used, it is clear that he understands his, and the peoples' suffering to be God's will for them at that time. He does not specifically address disability, but I suggest that people affected by disability often experience the same kinds of feelings as Jeremiah described, especially when the disability is first acquired or identified, and perhaps repeatedly during the course of life. Jeremiah spoke of being driven into darkness, besieged and surrounded with bitterness and hardship, being walled in and weighed down with heavy chains (vv. 2–7). Though he called out to God for help, he felt his prayers were shut out, his way blocked with stones and his paths made crooked (vv. 8–9). He used very descriptive words in relating his emotional/spiritual experience—dragged, mangled, made a target for arrows, pierced, made a laughingstock, filled with bitter herbs, teeth broken, trampled (vv. 10–16). In verses 17–18, he said his soul was bereft of peace so that he had forgotten what happiness is. Things seemed so bad that he exclaimed that his endurance and hope from the Lord had perished.

These are similar to emotions often expressed by families who have a child who is disabled. In part, these feelings arise from being unprepared to deal with disability, the loss of the child as they had envisioned during pregnancy, the "unknowns" about the child's development and potential functioning, and the prospect of having to care for the child throughout his or her life. Compounding this, is fear of what others will think about the child and the parents, what the response of others will be. Packer and Nystrom (2000) commented that "the death of hope has a killing effect on human hearts and minds" (p. 9). I believe that families dealing with disability often share Jeremiah's thoughts as they look on their situation, and are victims of that "killing effect." This underscores the need for the church to engage in disability ministry, creating a welcoming and supportive community. By coming alongside the family or individual, prayerfully providing spiritual care, and meeting their needs as God enables, the church can help those affected deepen their relationship with the Lord and inspire or rekindle hope in the God who "loves, redeems, pardons, restores, protects, keeps and uses misfits, outsiders and failures no less than he does beautiful people" (Packer & Nystrom, p. 24).

Jeremiah's story does not end with his despair. As if tethered on a leash by God, he is suddenly jerked back to spiritual reality and, in the midst of his lament, Jeremiah expresses renewed assurance:

> But this I call to mind, and therefore I have hope: The steadfast love of the LORD never ceases; his mercies never come to an end; they are new every morning; great is your faithfulness. 'The LORD is my portion,' says my soul, 'therefore I will hope in him' (Lamentations 3:21–24)

It is as if Jeremiah is suddenly reminded of who God is, thus renewing his hope. His hope was not wishful thinking, but a sureness that comes when turning his thoughts from his troubles to God. Fundamental in Jeremiah's mind was the realization that God's mercy and compassion will not—*cannot*—end because they are tied to his covenant faithfulness, God's integrity and inability to violate his own nature. Reflecting on his experience of God's faithfulness during his life (and Israel's life), renewed Jeremiah's confidence that God will complete all that he had promised.

To have God as our portion—our source of strength and blessing—is our only foundation for the hope that Jeremiah expressed, because God is faithful to himself, his promises, his word, and his covenant of grace and love. Our circumstances may change, as may our feelings about those circumstances, but God is unchanging. Our desire is that all who deal with disability come to this understanding. We want to assure them that "The LORD is good, a stronghold in the day of trouble; he knows those who take refuge in him" (Nahum 1:7). We want them to understand that disability is not stronger than God, nor can it prevent the person from knowing and serving God.

The stress of dealing with disability will not totally disappear. Situations will arise which raise the levels of individual and family stress from time to time (such as when other children are passing major developmental milestones or entering school, but their child still is unable to sit unsupported). Satan will exploit their fears and raise doubts as to God's love and faithfulness. At times we all have difficulty resting in the Lord. These are times when having the community of faith present in one's life is essential. Though depressing thoughts often make us desire to be alone, it is in the company of other believers that our "waiting" on the Lord is more doable.

> It is faith in our good and sovereign God that enables us to wait until the morning. But we must never forget that often the night is long and the weeping uncontrollable . . . . God's sovereignty doesn't take away the pain and evil that confront us in our lives; [he] works them for our good. (Schramek, 2006, p. 175)

"Christian faith is an expectant faith. It eagerly awaits the completion of the creative and redemptive activity of God" (Migliore, 2004, p. 330). But it is not solely hope in a distant future when God will complete the redemptive work in Christ. We do have that eternal perspective, an assurance of our resurrection and an eternity with Christ in the new heaven and earth. But Christian hope engenders energy, enthusiasm, and excitement for *today*. Christian hope is not blind optimism, but a confident assurance that centers on the unchanging character of God himself. More than just awaiting the fulfillment of God's promised restoration, at the heart of Christian hope is God's promise never to leave or forsake us (Deuteronomy 31:6; Hebrews 13:5)—a *present* promise that gives hope as we face the trials and difficulties of living in a fallen world. "Christian hoping, by virtue of its object (the guaranteed, never-ending generosity of God), calls forth love, joy, zeal, initiative and devoted *action*" (Packer & Nystrom, 2000, p. 14, emphasis added). An example of that "action" is the church's coming alongside families and individuals dealing with disability to actualize God's love by bringing comfort, as God has comforted us (2 Corinthians 1:4), and encouragement and needed help (2 Thessalonians 2:14), with the goal of stimulating hope in their hearts.

"Hope is a tender plant, easily crushed and extinguished" (Packer & Nystrom, p. 18). Families and individuals facing the issues related to disability are also tender plants, easily crushed by negative attitudes of others and by the difficulties associated with the impairment. Think again of the man in John 5—relatively isolated by the Pool of Bethesda, and having no one to help him. His only hope was to be the first into the pool should the waters be stirred, but he had no confidence in that hope. He was, using the biblical image, like a bruised, broken reed—an image representing the poor and oppressed (Barnes, n.d.). But the Suffering Servant was described in Isaiah 42:3 as one who "won't brush aside the bruised and the hurt and he won't disregard the small and insignificant, but he'll steadily and firmly set things right" (MSG). In Matthew 12:20, Jesus applies these words to himself, and this clearly showed in his earthly ministry. It must also be evident in our actions. Our own hope and confidence in God needs to "rub off" on those with whom we minister so that they also can see beyond the disability. Migliore (2004) pointed to the relationship between hope and ethics in these words:

> Genuine Christian hope—hope in the final triumph of God, in the completion of God's redemptive work in Christ, in God's promise of resurrection—moves and empowers believers to enter into real solidarity with afflicted humanity and with the whole groaning creation . . . . Christian hope does not close our eyes to the suffering of the world . . . . one of the most pressing challenges to people inside and outside the church today is to enter into an ever-widening circle of solidarity with all who suffer. (p. 349)

The Christian's hope should encourage and equip us, not just to wait for our Lord's return, but to do what we can, in the strength which God provides, to work for a world in which justice, freedom, and peace abound—especially, in our present focus, for people affected by disability.

Tips for the Church

David Benner (1998) wrote:

> If we rightly understand the revelation of the cross, we will understand that it is within suffering—our own and that of others—that Christ reveals himself . . . . Only when we stand with those who suffer pain, humiliation, starvation, and poverty and look at the world through their experience will we truly know the God who came into the world to share human pain. (p. 105)

Brenner suggested that there is a personal benefit to people who minister to others, as well as to the recipients of our ministry. But we must not go into this ministry for personal reward. The principle expressed in Jesus's statement about inviting guests to a banquet (Luke 14:12–14) is that our giving to others who are unable to repay makes God our "debtor," and we are assured of his repayment in the future. We do this ministry because of love for God, desire to obey his command, and a passion to bring honor *to* his name by living others *in* his name.

As we take the time to build a relationship with individuals and families affected by disability and come to understand their needs, abilities, and dreams, we are better able to come alongside and provide the spiritual, pastoral care that will promote their own spiritual maturation. Getting to know the family—listening to their stories, their history and experience to understand their needs—takes time and repeated contact, but is essential. Through this contact, we become more aware of the stresses and struggles they deal with, and may be able to identify their spiritual needs, such as assurance of forgiveness, acceptance, and the love of God; the need for relatedness and hope; and an understanding of the dignity and worth of even the most severely disabled individual. We are then able to more specifically pray with them about these issues, provide appropriate spiritual/pastoral care, and work with them to discover or create means of providing the kind of support needed. One of the most important aspects of spiritual/pastoral care is to assure the individual and family, perhaps repeatedly, of God's unconditional love—which may best be taught through our own unconditional love for them.

Along with being present to the individuals and families, especially in times of crisis, our ministry needs to find ways for them to be integrated into the church family. This can broaden their support system as they develop additional friendships, spiritually feed them as they share in worship and Bible study, provide a bit of respite as others care for their children, and allow them to use their talents and gifts to serve others and the Lord.

In ministering to and with individuals and families affected by disability, we must also recognize that they may have many capabilities and inherent strengths that remain untapped and need to be developed. Churches need to provide opportunities for disabled individuals to connect with and contribute positively to the family, community, and the church. Spiritual/pastoral care can be reciprocal—able-bodied persons are not always the ministers; people with disabilities may also minister to us, through their example of courage and dependence on God, and through the exercise of their natural talents and spiritual gifts.

Central to everything we do is the desire to share God's love and to lead the individual and family into a new or deeper relationship with God. For individuals or families not already believers, whether or not they become followers of Christ is in God's hands; our charge is to show Christ to the world through our actions and words, and to love our neighbors regardless of how they respond to that offer of love. Jesus is our model, both for action and attitude. Jesus willingly submitted to the Father's will, making himself vulnerable by taking on human form and living in conditions of poverty under Roman rule, and opening his arms on Calvary to offer the embrace of forgiveness and peace to all who would come to him. As his representatives, his ministers, we must show the same willingness to embrace others in Christ's name, lovingly and compassionately offering acceptance and welcome.

As individuals, we all have an important part to play in demonstrating the gospel through our lives. We can pray, give, volunteer, and become effective personal ambassadors for the gospel. However, our greatest power to change the world is released when we come together in collective action to organize and focus the resources of the whole body of Christ. (Stearns, 2010, p. 179)

Going Deeper

1. How would your life be different had you, or your child been born with a disability? What spiritual and emotional issues would you have faced when the diagnosis was first made?

2. The chapter referred to person-centered, family-centered, socially-centered, and spiritually-centered factors which produce or intensify stress within the family. How can you or your church help alleviate some of these stress factors?

3. What are some concrete ways you can embody hope to people who are dealing with issues of disability?

4. Christ saw value and significance in people that were dismissed or ignored by his culture. Even Christ himself was "despised and rejected" (Isaiah 53:3). James 2:5 could easily apply to persons and families facing issues of disability. But if God has chosen them to be rich in faith and heirs of the kingdom, how are we (the Church) to respond?

5. Zechariah 7:9–10 reads, "Thus says the LORD of hosts, Render true judgments, show kindness and mercy to one another, do not oppress the widow, the fatherless, the sojourner, or the poor, and let none of you devise evil against another in your heart." People who are disabled fit into the groups listed in this passage. How can you (and your church) show kindness and mercy to people and families dealing with disability? What behaviors qualify as "oppression" and "devising evil"? Does this refer only to active behaviors toward the people, or is lack of action also a form of oppression? When have you advocated or acted to bring justice to people with disabilities? What are some other Scripture passages that speak of doing justice on the behalf of marginalized people?

6. In 2 Corinthians 5:16, Paul says "From now on, therefore, we regard no one according to the flesh. Even though we once regarded Christ according to the flesh, we regard him thus no longer." Explain how this relates to disability issues.

Chapter Seven

A Biblical Understanding
of Health and Healing

In chapter two, I referred to Jean Vanier, founder of L'Arche, a network of small Christian homes for people with disabilities now found in many communities around the world. Vanier believed that weakness is a precious gift and that our welcoming of those who are vulnerable brings spiritual nourishment to both giver and recipient. He wrote, "It is important to bring broken people into a community of love, a place where they feel accepted and recognized in their gifts, and have a sense of belonging. That is what wounded people need and want" (Vanier, 1992, p. 28). I believe the Church should be identified as such a place. This requires that Christians have a proper understanding of disability and of the opportunity God has given us to demonstrate the Gospel through ministry. It also requires that Christians understand the "value" of vulnerability and weakness (chapter four), and have a biblical view of health and healing. We begin by exploring the relationship between sin and disease or disability.

Biblical View of Health

Many Christians incorrectly believe that a "whole body" signifies God's love and blessing, and that a "disabled body" indicates God's judgment for sin. This was the attitude conveyed by Job's three counselors, and it is the thought behind the question asked by Jesus's disciples regarding the man born blind (John 9). To be sure, there are biblical passages which *appear* to link disease and disability with sin (e.g., Leviticus 26; Luke 5:18–26), but we must be careful not to divorce these passages from the whole counsel of God. In Leviticus 26, blessings are listed for those who obey God, and punishment, often quite severe, is said to follow disobedience. Disability, however, is not directly included as part of the punishment. Viewing this passage in light of the entirety of God's Word suggests that Christians who do _not_ show love and compassion to persons with disability, but instead unjustly marginalize, ignore, or discriminate against them, should experience God's punishment. And the Luke 5 passage must be radically twisted to read any connection between the man's disability and personal sin. If personal sin results in disability, everyone should be disabled!

Richards (1999) explained that the New Testament associates illness and disease (and, by extension, disability) in general with forces hostile to God and to humanity. That is, these weaknesses of humanity were not what God intended at creation; they reflect humanity's alienation from God as a result of the fall (Genesis 3). As evidence of the sentence of death that followed the Fall, sickness and disability are broadly connected with "Sin" which had entered the world following our first parents' disobedience, but it was not connected with the personal sin of an individual (cf. John 9:1–3). Jesus's attitude and actions reveal God's desire to be our healer, not our punisher. "To see illness or disability only as punishment misreads both the nature of God and the nature of the satanic forces that distort human experience (Richards, 1999, p. 564).

We often hear people speak of human beings as consisting of body and soul and spirit. Biblically speaking, we are all of these things in unity; they are all aspects of our "person." To think of them as separate can distort our understanding of what it means to be human—each must be understood with reference to the other. When we act, for example, it is not simply the body or the mind that acts; it is the totality of our being that acts and is responsible before God. The "parts" of our being (body, soul, spirit) do not operate in opposition to one another anymore than our hands and feet act in opposition (cf. 1 Corinthians 12:12–26).

We are eternal beings temporarily residing in a physical body. But that physical body is subject to illness, accidents, and the effects of ageing or of improper care and nutrition. The Bible tells us that we will receive new bodies in heaven (Romans 8:10–11) and places emphasis on the soul as that which is eternal. Physical health or wholeness of body is not the highest virtue or value (cf. Matthew 5:29–30; 6:25–27; 10:28). This requires that we rethink "health" and "wholeness" from a biblical perspective.

Most people think of "healthy" as being able to perform daily life activities so as to maintain themselves. The emphasis is on *doing*. The biblical idea of health, however, is more holistic and derives from the concept of shalom, understood as wholeness and delight. It has more to do with healthy relationships than freedom from disease or disability (Shelly, 2000). Biblical health can be thought of as a state in which people's needs are met and they are able to use their natural gifts, all under the canopy of God's love. Central to this "health" is a person's sense of *being* in the community.

The difficulty, then, lies in how temporarily able-bodied persons regard those who have a disability. The significant problem faced by people who had an impairment in Jesus's day was that the disability interfered with their participation in the community. They tended to be devalued and excluded, as was the man in John 5. (The same situation is faced by many persons with disabilities today, particularly in less developed nations.) The exclusion was the result of inappropriate understanding and attitudes regarding disease and disability and concern for the effect they would have on the order and functioning of the community. Sickness or disability thus disrupted relationships and created a sense of alienation and isolation on the part of those affected (Black, 1996). The focus on community integrity did not encourage support for the individual but led to exclusion and devaluation. The community then drew boundaries to ensure protection—not for the person who was ill or disabled, but for the rest of the community. Rejection by the social and religious communities experienced by people with disabilities in biblical times was not so much based on the assumption they had committed a sinful act, but simply because of some aspect of who they were, some part of their *being*, in this case, their disability

In Mark 10:46–52, for example, we meet Bartimaeus, whose visual impairment resulted in his living as a beggar. We are told that he is "sitting by the side of the road," very likely by the gutter, where people would discard rubbish. The crowds attempted to silence him when he called out to Jesus. Unlike the crowds, Jesus did not push Bartimaeus aside but displayed a welcoming attitude.

Jesus ordered someone to bring Bartimaeus to him. This immediately changed how Bartimaeus was viewed by the people—since Jesus took time to speak with him, perhaps Bartimaeus has more value than was thought! Jesus treated Bartimaeus with respect, elicited a profession of belief from him, and told Bartimaeus his faith led to his being made well.[7] His blindness was instantly cured but, more importantly, Bartimaeus was *healed*, both positionally and spiritually. Positionally, because having his sight restored led to his reinstatement as part of the community. Mark tells us Bartimaeus joined the group of travelers to Jerusalem. Spiritual healing was evidenced by his joining the group of disciples (Luke 18:43 adds that he followed Jesus and glorified God). Bartimaeus no longer sat alone by the side of the road; now he walked in the Way.

Biblical health does not preclude having some limitation. Moses may have had a speech impediment (Exodus 4:10), Paul had "a thorn in the flesh" (2 Corinthians 12:7–10); Timothy had frequent stomach ailments (1 Timothy 5:23); Ephaphoditus experienced a serious illness and "nearly died for the work of the Lord" (Philippians 2:25–30). Yet none of these "limitations" precluded God's ability to further the development of his kingdom through these men. God can, and often does, work through illness or disability. As God told Paul, it is in human weakness that God's power is made perfect (2 Corinthians 12:9). A biblical view of health does not focus on bodily function or the ability to be "in control" of one's life, however. Scripturally, health is well-being, as in the sense of shalom.

Cure versus Healing

It is necessary to recognize the distinction between the words *cure* and *heal*. Longchar (2011) explained the difference this way: "'Cure' refers to bodily, developmental, and psychological restoration to what is considered normal. In contrast, 'healing' refers to a sense of well-being that encompasses attitudinal and emotional health" (p. 55). Cure pertains to the elimination of at least the symptoms, if not the disease or the disability itself. This was actually rare in biblical times, and generally not expected, making Jesus's miracles all the more significant. To heal, on the other hand, centers on evoking a sense of well-being, peace, comfort, and support, but does *not* imply a cure. Isaiah 53:5, for example, says that "the punishment that brought us *peace* was upon him, and by his wounds we are *healed*." The "peace" is shalom—the well-being, completeness, and reconciliation that Christ provides. "Healed" refers to our being made *whole* in spirit; that is, our healing from sin—release from bondage to and the consequences of sin (Romans 5:8–11, 6:1–6; Galatians 5:1).

The true focus of Jesus's activity was on healing more than curing—his atoning sacrifice did not bring freedom from illness, accidents, or disability; it brought us from the kingdom of darkness into the kingdom of light (1 Peter 2:9). The man in John 9 whose blindness was cured ended up being excommunicated by the Jewish leaders. (Notice that the leaders of the synagogue again missed the point. They could not deny that the man was no longer blind; their focus

---

[7] Note the contrast: Bartimaeus, in his blindness, knew who Jesus was, calling him "Jesus, Son of David"—a name with both covenant and messianic significance. The crowds, however, referred to him only as "Jesus of Nazareth." And, to the leaders of the Jews, Jesus was thought a blasphemer leading them to seek his extermination.

was on the fact that his curing had occurred on the Sabbath, just like with the man in John 5.) Although the Pharisees expelled the once-blind man from the synagogue, the man was restored to community and fellowship through his faith in Jesus. This spiritual restoration—*healing*—was ultimately what Jesus referred to when he said the man's blindness was "so that the work of God might be displayed in his life" (John 9:4). Similarly, in Mark 2, the man with a severe physical disability lowered through the roof to the feet of Jesus first had his spiritual needs met: Jesus forgave his sin. Then, Jesus cured the man of his disability as a sign to the Scribes and others of his authority. In neither of these cases was sin the cause of the disability. Curing the disability pointed to who Jesus is.

Curing was an important part of Christ's ministry. He displayed both his power and authority by curing people who were sick, disabled, or demon-possessed. This served to authenticate his teaching and preaching, to prove that he was from God. Jesus did not require faith on the part of a person, certainly not as a requirement for being cured. Luke 17:11–19 tells of ten men with leprosy who called to Jesus from a distance, "Jesus, Master, have mercy on us." Their cry to Jesus signifies their understanding that Jesus has the power to cure their skin disease. "Master" in Greek is *epistates*, meaning chief commander; it does not, however, indicate recognition of Jesus as Lord. Jesus gave no message of curing, but simply told them to do as the law required: present themselves to the priests to verify their cleansing (Leviticus 14:1–32). On their way to do as Jesus instructed, the men realized they had become clean. But only one—a Samaritan (presumably the others were all Jews)—returned to offer thanks. To him, Jesus said, "your faith has made you well," using the more comprehensive word *sozo*, meaning *saved* or *made whole*. Only this man returned to praise Jesus and thus received this greater blessing. But the implied absence of faith in the other nine men did not result in being reinfected with the skin disease.

Jesus cured many who were physically ill or disabled, but the greater focus of his ministry was on people's *spiritual* "disease and disability." His message was not "come to me and be cured," but focused on the good news of the Kingdom of God. Jesus's words offered freedom, hope, peace of heart, and eternal life with God—the true message of healing. His miracles showed him to be the true King, with authority over evil powers and earthly disease and disability, and carried with them the promise of complete renewal at his return, as Paul talks about in Romans 8:18–25. The purpose for which Jesus came into the world was to demonstrate through his death and resurrection his power and authority to conquer sin and restore people to a right relationship with God and with others—the kind of *healing* that is needed by both the temporarily able-bodied and persons with disabilities.

The Kingdom had come with Jesus the King, but the Kingdom is not yet fully here. The miracles of Jesus's ministry provided a foretaste of what will be experienced when the new heaven and earth is established, when there will no longer be sickness, disability, or sin. Thus, physical curing is not the most important gift God can give. We must be careful not to concentrate on God's power to remove sickness and disability more than on his authority to forgive sin. After all, which is more important: having a "whole" body now yet being bound for hell, or having a disabled body now but be destined for eternity with Christ? Jesus saw spiritual health and wholeness as more important than physical health and bodily wholeness. Humankind's spiritual state was Jesus's first concern, and this must be our primary focus. Complete healing will occur in Christ's coming kingdom, but to be "in" that kingdom, people must first come to know Jesus.

Miracles do still occur, especially the miracle of childbirth and the miracle of spiritual rebirth (a re-creative act of God). God still brings about physical cure—sometimes through special (miraculous) intervention, and sometimes by using human means (medical doctors, medications). But God's desire is to use his Church to bring *healing* (restoration, reconciliation, relationship). We must keep in mind that the physical aspect of a disability is not what needs healing the most. To live without the limitations of a disability might be desired, but the social isolation and alienation experienced by people with disabilities is a larger problem, one which suggests that healing is needed in the hearts and attitudes of both persons with disabilities and those who are temporarily able-bodied—a problem most in need of God's gracious healing through the church.

Is "Cure" Necessary?

In chapter one, I wrote that people with disabilities and people who are temporarily able-bodied have more commonalities than differences. Vulnerability is one of these common elements—all humankind is vulnerable to illness and accidents, some of which could result in disability. Weakness is also common to all people—we each have things at which we excel and things which we do less well. Though weakness, at least temporary or intermittent, is part of the experience of every human being we generally seek to keep our limitations or weaknesses hidden. But this weakness is not necessarily a negative factor as it encourages interdependence—our need of others (illustrated by Paul as he compared the human body with the church in 1 Corinthians 12)—as well as our dependence upon God.

When encountering a person with an obvious physical or mental impairment, however, some believe that person needs to be made healthy through a cure. This has contributed to the development of medical, physical, and educational treatments which have enabled people with disabilities to function more effectively and independently. But for some this as insufficient; what they believe is needed is what they call "faith healing." The problem is that overemphasis on the need for a cure to disability or serious illness overlooks the fact that *care* is often more important than *cure* and discounts the fact that everyone deserves love. The Bible teaches that all people have worth because they are created as God's image, regardless of ability or disability. Christian love is not restricted to those who have conventional bodies and minds, making it a priority that we communicate that each person deserves love and inclusion (Edmonds, 2011). The fullness of God's love, and Jesus's atoning death, are for all people without concern about physical, mental, or psychological limitation. A proper Christian response is to comfort those who are vulnerable or suffering.

Narrow ideas about the need for "cure" and the subsequent abandonment of the individual if cure is not forthcoming after a time of concerted prayer often lead to isolation of the person rather than to a deepening of love and compassion. There is at least an implied accusation that the person lacks faith or has failed to confess sin (just as Job's counselors claimed). Rather than being drawn into closer relationship with God and the family of Christ, our actions may convey to the person that he or she is not "good enough" to be a part of our fellowship, leading to feelings of hopelessness. Such rejection displays a negative attitude toward limitation and disability which may then be attached to the individual. Actually, those judging the person give evidence not only of their own sinfulness, but also their lack of faith—faith that God can bring good out of situations we see as bad; faith that God can use even the most severely disabled person to accomplish his purposes; faith that disability cannot prevent God from loving someone; faith that recognizes, as did Paul, that God's grace is sufficient, that God's power is made perfect in our weakness.

We must remember that Jesus did not require his followers to first be without limitation or weakness or sin before they were acceptable; in fact, it was while we were still weak, still sinners, still enemies that Christ died for us (Romans 5:6–10). We have no basis for judging someone unworthy or unacceptable because they are disabled or remain disabled after we have prayed earnestly for God to cure them. God cures according to his will, not our demand. We must not overlook the fact that Jesus did not cure everyone during his earthly ministry, but was selective in bringing a cure to people. In John 5, for example, Jesus focused on the man who had been disabled for 38 years. There were probably many others with various forms and degrees of disability or disease lying by the pool of Bethesda hoping to be first into the water, yet Jesus ministered only to this man. Mark 1:29–38 relates that in the evening "the whole city" gathered and Jesus healed many. Early the next morning the disciples told Jesus everyone was looking for him—most likely meaning others who were sick or disabled. Jesus's response, however, was to move on: "Let us go on the next town that I may preach there also, for that is why I came" (Mark 1:38). On another occasion, Jesus said the poor will always be present (Matthew 26:11). Linking this thought to Jesus's words in Matthew 25:31–46, we can assume that the same is true of people who are sick, disabled, imprisoned, etc. There will be no permanent cure for all disease or disability in this world.

Nick Vujicic (2010) was born without arms or legs. There was a time when he prayed that God would give him limbs, thinking that this would give him joy and purpose. He said "I was never crippled until I lost hope. Believe me, the loss of hope is far worse than the loss of limbs" (p. 46). Nick has been used by God throughout the world to bring a message of hope to people who are suffering emotionally, physically, or psychologically. Nick wrote that God took his life and gave it meaning and purpose and joy, without curing his disability, and stated "I'm officially *disabled*, but I'm truly *enabled* because of my lack of limbs. My unique challenges have opened up unique opportunities to reach so many in need" (p. 2). Christians must recognize that insistence on a cure may actually limit what God can do through the person who is disabled by creating discouragement and despair.

Is Disability Related to Personal Sin?

To assume that all disability is sin-related, and that not being cured in response to prayer represents lack of faith on the part of a person, is to "blame the victim," and can lead to avoidance and exclusion. Some might even conclude that the person got what he or she deserved because of assumed sin or faithlessness. Such reasoning places us in the position of being judge, a position which only God can occupy. In making these judgments, we fail to realize that our attitude can cause suffering on the part of the person with the disability, while at the same time making us guilty of disobeying God's command to love our neighbor and Christ's command to bring the gospel to every people group.

To say that God is punishing a person by giving them a child with a disability, or by allowing them to become disabled, is a form of *spiritual abuse,* and reflects an incorrect understanding of our position, of God, and of sin. First, based as it is on human judgment, the one who pronounces that the disability is because of a person's (or the parent's) sin conveys the idea that he or she is more righteous than the one judged. This violates the principle of humility and unconditional love which Jesus displayed and commanded. Secondly, it misrepresents God, who acts lovingly toward his children, not punitively (though he does allow us to experience the logical consequences of our actions). The Bible tells us that God's love is such that he gave his only Son to redeem the world, even while we were his enemies (John 3:16; Romans 5:10). If Jesus was not sent to judge the world (John 3:17), why would he _now_ judge or punish people's sin with disability? Judgment is reserved for Jesus's return (Acts 17:31; 2 Corinthians 5:10). To insist that disability is God's punishment for personal sin or the parents' sin, does not convey the *good news* of the Gospel. Thirdly, to assert that disability is punishment for sin reveals an incorrect understanding of the universality of sin, and implies that the person making the judgment believes he or she to be without sin since God has not disabled them. It is like telling the person dealing with disability, "I am right with God because I am not disabled, but you are not."

Believing the person is experiencing the just rewards of sin, or that God is using disability to lead them to repentance, results in pressure being applied to confess sin, with the implication that God will then remove the disability (which, depending of the nature of the disability, would require God to alter the chromosomal structure of the entire body, replace a missing limb, repair damaged neural cells, or reverse the effect of ageing). Like Job, personal sin is _not_ always the reason for illness, disability, or suffering. Can God only be God if he cures disability or disease? If so, why did he not cure Paul of his "thorn in the flesh"?

It bears repeating: the primary need of diseased or disabled people is not a "cure." Wholeness (shalom) does not require a conventional body or mental facility. Jesus said that he came so that people would have abundant life (John 10:10b), but his reference was not to physical or economic abundance; he was speaking about spiritual life. For us to be "full" or "whole" spiritually, to have abundant spiritual life, does not require being free of disease or disability. To overly focus on curing emphasizes the wrong thing—our body or physical health. Jesus is more concerned with healthy spirits/souls. Insisting on cure is _not_ seeing things as God sees them, and _not_ seeing people and disabilities as God does. We are in no position to dictate to God what he must do. And we certainly must not reject the person if cure does not happen. We are not to blame the person for unconfessed sin or lack of faith, thereby doing more harm to the person's spirit. God can redeem any experience, displaying in the life of someone who is disabled his own wondrous working. God's work *can* be to cure the person—God is the source of health and wholeness—but it can also be displayed by enriching the disabled person with endurance and a spirit of praise.

Matthew 8 gives an account of Jesus ministering to people's physical needs—curing a man who had leprosy, the paralyzed servant of a Centurion, and Peter's mother-in-law, who was sick with a fever (possibly malaria). Verses 16–17 provide an interesting insight into Jesus's healing power. We read that many who were oppressed by demons or sick were brought to Jesus so that he could cure them. According to Matthew, Jesus's actions were a fulfillment of Isaiah's prophecy: "He took our illnesses and bore our diseases" (Isaiah 53:4). Wiersbe (2001a) observed that this indicates that the prophecy was fulfilled in Jesus's *life*, not solely by his death on the cross. Jesus's life and ministry were important aspects of Jesus's mission. His curing people who were "bound" by sickness or disability demonstrated Jesus's authority more than his power, and were indicative of his mission to proclaim good news to the poor, liberty to the captives, recovery of sight to the blind, and set at liberty those who are oppressed (Luke 4:18), all consequences of Adam's sin. God is obligated to save all who repent of sin and call Jesus "Lord," but he is *not* obligated to cure all sicknesses or disabilities in this life. Any cure that is received in this life is only temporary, anyway—even Lazarus died a second time.

Is faith required for cure? Sometimes we read in the Gospels that a miracle occurred when there was little or no faith (e.g., Jesus's calming the sea, Matthew 8:26). Other times, faith is the result, not the stimulus for a cure (e.g., Matthew 15:31). It is essential that we believe in God as a healer, but we must accept that curing disability is solely the sovereign will of God; it does not necessarily depend upon a person's faith (Onyinab, 2006).

For Christians to overly emphasize the need for the disability to be cured can even be a form of idolatry (Hittenberger & Mittelstadt, 2008) and unintentionally reinforce feelings of isolation or stigma on the part of the disabled person. Telling people that their disability is the result of personal sin may lead to shame, guilt, and unworthiness. If they have confessed sin but not been cured, they at best become frustrated, but at worst develop a view of God as angry and unforgiving (especially if they cannot think of "the sin" which resulted in their becoming disabled). This can cause them not to seek help or to believe that they are unworthy of a relationship with God or with non disabled persons. Warrington (2006) made this important point about the healing ministry of Jesus:

> . . . the most important lesson is to recognize that the authors of the gospels described the healings in order that Jesus should be exalted in the minds of the readers. The stories were not told to encourage us to emulate Jesus and thus enable us to be healers as he was; his healings were unique and were associated with his unique mission. In healing, he demonstrated an authority that belongs to God. (p. 158)

Disabled God?

Some writers have referred to Jesus as "the disabled God" (cf. Eiesland, 1994; Cooper, 1992). This is strong language, and some believers are uncomfortable with the phrase, but this metaphorical way of thinking of Christ can deepen our understanding of God's redemptive love and grace. It is important to recognize that our Lord and Savior was himself broken—disabled—in order to bring about salvation for humankind. As Longchar (2011, p. 43) stated, "The image of the wounded God illustrates that even though the body may be wounded, the image never loses a given wholeness—the wholeness of the divine in whose image the human being is made" (p. 43).

Moltmann (1998) wrote that the healing power of Jesus flows from his ability to suffer; healing comes through fellowship with God:

In Jesus Christ, God himself became Man. He took on complete, real humanity and made it part of his own divine life. The eternal God took on not only the limited and mortal aspects of humanity but also the disabled, sick, weak, helpless, and lifeless aspects of humanity. He took on our disabilities and made them part of his eternal life. He takes on our tears and makes them an expression of his own pain. It is by taking on every sickness and every care and making them his own sufferings and his own cares that God heals all sicknesses and all cares. (p. 116)

Implications for the Christian Community

Jesus did not make "curing" a requirement for being accepted into the family of God. Neither should we. The ministry of Jesus should encourage us to pray to God for physical cure, but we must "continue to trust him to bring good out of every situation, *whether he cures or not*" (Onyinab, 2006, p. 126, emphasis added). This accords with Paul's teaching in Romans 8:28, "we know that for those who love God all things work together for good, for those who are called according to his purpose."

> The Christian approach to severe suffering and disability is to provide for the easing of pain and anxiety . . . and support for spiritual and social healing, in a caring environment where patients are reassured of their value and quality . . . . Dignity is found when a caring society supports those in greatest need, and ensures that everyone, whatever their disability, is persuaded of their value to society. (Edwards, 2000, pp. 15–16)

The Church must bring healing through acceptance, support, and encouragement—not create or endorse boundaries to protect itself from those considered "unclean or cursed." We must guard against the idea that a person needs to be made physically and mentally "whole," through miracle or medicine, in order to be an active participant in the life of the church. We must not assume that the person's most urgent need is to be physically cured. God is able to use a person in his or her disabled state to bring glory to himself, perhaps even more so *because* of that person's "weakness." From a Christian standpoint, therefore, disability is not necessarily something to be gotten rid of. It can actually be a tool or a vessel for God to bring blessing to people (cf. Paul's "thorn in the flesh" in 2 Corinthians 12:9); to bring glory to himself, not through curing, but through healing; or as a means of testifying to his grace and provision.

It is imperative for the Church to recognize and promote the idea that difference must be honored and accepted. Focus, for ourselves and for the person who is disabled, must be on transformation toward Christlikeness and healing of spirit, more than fixing the body. The role of the entire Christian community in this transformation is critical.

Christians must be people of hope, but this hope is found in Christ and the promise of being in his presence for eternity—not wealth and health in this world. In the Beatitudes (Matthew 5:3–10), Jesus said God blesses those who are poor in spirit, who mourn, who are meek, who hunger and thirst for righteousness, who are merciful and pure in heart, who are peacemakers, and who are persecuted for the sake of righteousness. The word blessed (*makarios*) in these verses refers to inner satisfaction and sufficiency that is not dependent on our outward circumstances for happiness (Wiersbe, 2001a). God's blessing is comfort, satisfaction, mercy, becoming children of God, and being part of God's kingdom. There is no promise of a life of physical health and wealth. Health and prosperity teaching is based on a false belief that *we* are in control. Beneath that thinking is fear, not hope. Such thinking denies the reality of life in a fallen world. Dahlstrom's (2011) comment is relevant:

> The good life is never defined by Jesus in terms of either length or comfort. To the contrary, Jesus says that those who seek to save their life will lose it, and those who lose their lives, spilling them out generously in service to others because of love for God and humanity, will find them . . . . fullness isn't defined by Jesus in terms of length but in terms of depth. (pp. 127–128)

Obtaining a cure for physical illness or disability does not supercede the need to experience God's love, expressed through his people. By offering unconditional love and acceptance to persons who are disabled, Christians promote healing which enables people dealing with disability to realize their human wholeness even in the absence of physical cure (Hittenberger & Mittelstadt, 2008). Temporarily able-bodied people may tend to think that the primary desire of someone who is disabled is to be cured. But, especially if the disabled person is a Christian, while a cure may be welcomed, the greater need is to be welcomed as a friend, a brother or sister in Christ, and to be given opportunity to actively participate to the faith community.

Joni Eareckson Tada has lived with a disability for over 40 years. She views disability as Satan's "last great stronghold to defame the good character of God. Suffering is that last frontier he exploits to smear God's trustworthiness" (Tada, 2010, p. 30). She suggested that the real question is not *whether* God can or does cure, but whether or not God *wills* to cure everyone who comes to him in faith. Sometimes God will cure a person of disease or disability immediately and miraculously. But often, for purposes know only to God, he will withhold a cure while at the same time working within the heart of a believer who is disabled to bring healing in a larger sense. The Bible does not teach that God will cure all who come to him in faith, but it does affirm that God "sovereignly reserves the right to heal or not heal, as He sees fit" (Tada, 2010, p. 45).

It is important that the Church be seen as a place of grace. Part of this is to be certain that individuals dealing with issues of disability are not made to feel that the disability is because of sin. Even if a person did become disabled as the unintended result of sinful behavior (such as binge drinking that lead to an auto accident that leaves them paralyzed), our responsibility as Christians is not to judge and shun but to love and comfort the person in Jesus's name. Our focus must be on their needs as people made in the image of God. We are to do what we can to "enact the grace of God" (Edmonds, 2011)—promoting their well-being and helping them to flourish despite the limitations caused by disability. We must not add suffering to their experience by concluding that they received what they deserved or by rejecting or ignoring them because they are disabled. Building trust within a personal relationship requires time and effort. Christians must be ready to make that investment, nurturing friendships and providing pastoral care, thereby reducing or countering the stigma often associated with disability.

Beates (2012) concluded:

> The absence of people with disabilities in the church indicates that the church has not yet grasped deeply enough the essence of the gospel; and conversely, God's people have drunk

too deeply from the well of cultural ideology with regard to wholeness and brokenness. If people with disabilities are not welcomed by the church, much less aggressively pursued by the church, it may be because, like the world around us, we would rather think we are on the way to recovery, that we are strong in Christ and healthy. We would rather not be bothered by the care that those who live with brokenness require. We don't wish to be reminded by their very presence how much like them we really are. (p. 79)

The particular aspects of Jesus's ministry were expressions of his love for the Father and for humankind. Preaching and demonstrating this love was central to his life, death, and resurrection. They must also be marks of the Christian Church today.

Going Deeper

1. Spend time meditating on Isaiah 53:3–5. Verse 3 speaks about being left, or forsaken by people, no longer being regarded as a human being—not even worthy of being noticed. This is similar to the way people with disabilities are often regarded. Note the "disability" terms used in verses 4–5: *Infirmities:* physical pain involving bodily infirmity, disability, disease. *Sorrows:* pains of the mind: anguish, anxiety, or trouble of the soul. *Pierced:* literally "to bore" as in the drilling of a bore-hole. *Crushed:* being crumbled or broken into pieces. *Wounds:* the welts on Jesus's flesh as a result of flogging. With nails through his hands and feet, Jesus was "disabled" on the cross; paralyzed—unable to move except his head and to push up with feet to breathe. *How does this affect your view of disabilities and of the disabled?*

   Longchar (2011) commented, "As the incarnate God, Jesus presents the image of a disabled God . . . A powerfully illustrated ministry of Jesus is not in his healing of broken bodies and restoring sanity to the possessed *but more so in his embrace of disability*" (p. 42, emphasis added). He suggested that the words of Isaiah 53 demonstrate that our socially constructed ideas of perfection, superiority, inferiority and functionality give shape to a warped theological view of disability. *Do you agree or disagree with Longchar?*

2. What suggestions do the following verses give about relating with people who have disabilities and their families?

   a. James 1:2–3

   b. 1 Corinthians 9:22–23

3. How does the following verse suggest that disability can be part of God's plan for a person, rather than God's curse or punishment? "In Christ we were chosen to be God's people, because from the very beginning God had decided this in keeping with his plan. And he is the One who makes everything agree with what he decides and wants." (Ephesians 1:11, NCV)

4. Based on passages such as 2 Corinthians 12:7–10, Galatians 4:13–15, and Galatians 6:11, Yong (2011) wondered whether Paul may have been the first theologian with a disability. Paul uses the word *astheneia* in 2 Corinthians 12:9 and 10 to describe his condition. As we saw in chapter one, astheneia is generally translated as "weakness" but also describes infirmity or disease. It is probably "the closest ancient Greek parallel to the modern term 'disability'" (Albl quoted in Yong, p. 84). What is your response to this suggestion? Does it change your evaluation of Paul? Of disability?

Chapter Eight

Disability and the Problem of Evil and Suffering

Christians should be quick to minister to individuals and families dealing with disabilities—but the church has largely overlooked this population. Some believe people with disabilities are not worth the effort (or that they are simply reaping the results of personal sin, or that they are "cursed"). Most people lack both information about disabilities and exposure to people with disabilities. Many do not know how to reconcile their understanding of God as loving and merciful with the existence of disabling conditions. *To ignore the existence of disabilities is to deny reality; to ignore people with disabilities is to be unchristlike.*

Worldview Challenge

Christians may be asked how they reconcile God's creativity, sovereignty, righteousness, and love with the existence of people with disabilities in our world. The occurrence of disabilities may challenge people's understanding of and belief in the biblically revealed God. Their concept of justice may be shaken when a person becomes disabled or is born with a disability. They may question God's wisdom, or at least doubt Paul's teaching in Romans 8:28 about God working things for the good of those who love him. People may wonder about the usefulness to God of a person who is or becomes disabled. For believers, a disabling condition may cause a *crisis of faith*—how can we reconcile the goodness of God with the "suffering" caused by the disability? The issue may not be a question of whether God truly exists, but about trusting God in such circumstances. The confusion revolves around understanding God's purpose.

"Theodicy" is the technical term for how Christians have attempted to respond to these issues; how they try to deal with the problem of evil and suffering so evident in our world. The classical expression of the "problem of evil" reads like this:

> If God is all-good, he would will all good and no evil. If God is all-powerful, he would accomplish everything he wills. But evil exists as well as good. Therefore, God either is not all-powerful or not all-good—or does not exist at all.

The issue becomes more clouded when considering moral evil versus natural evil (disasters in nature, for example), and the quantity and intensity of evil as we see it on almost a daily basis. There are two dimensions involved which are important in how we might respond to someone who raises the problem of evil with us. At one level, the question is theological or philosophical in nature, making it more academic and abstract. At another level, the question is religious or existential—personal and real in the life of individuals and families. Several theological and philosophical answers have been proposed. They are not mutually exclusive, but overlap in many aspects. Each contributes to our understanding of suffering; each explains some aspect of, or type of suffering and evil. While these explanations help in an abstract sense, they give little or no comfort to people who are in the midst of suffering (the religious or existential level).

Answering the Problem: Free-Will

One way the problem has been addressed is called the "free-will defense." It begins by making the assertion that evil is not a "thing"—it has no positive nature. Evil is not something coeternal with God, nor something God created. Rather, evil is the absence, or loss, of something good. It is disordered love or will, stemming from a wrong relationship between people and God which began with Adam and Eve's disobedience.

God is absolutely perfect and created only perfect beings. But for humankind to be "perfect," required the ability to freely choose good or evil. Human freedom did not mean complete or absolute autonomy; Adam and Eve were morally responsible before their Creator to obey his instructions and fulfill the purpose for which they were created: to love God and bring glory to him. The exercise of their free choice to disobey rather than to honor God, brought sin and evil into the world. The *potential* for evil was always there (given Adam's ability to freely choose), but evil did not become *actual* until Genesis 3, when Eve was deceived by the serpent and Adam chose to disobey God. Having made that choice, humankind became separated from God and our sin-nature came into being, holding humankind in spiritual captivity.

As a result of Adam and Eve's disobedience, God cursed the serpent, Satan, and the ground (but not Adam and Eve). The word used in Genesis 3 for "curse" is the Hebrew word *arar*. Richards (1999) explained that this word means to bind something in a way that reduces its ability or renders it powerless. As a consequence of Adam and Eve's disobedience, the earth was cursed—its "original spontaneous fertility" was reduced so that it is no longer able to produce as originally created and humankind is unable to enjoy the earth's produce without toilsome labor (Richards, 1999, p. 207). Paul, in Romans 8:20–23, spoke of all creation being subjected to futility and bondage, corruption and decay. The divine order was disrupted; what in Genesis 2 seemed peaceful and idyllic had changed. What God had told Adam would ensue if the command not to eat the fruit of the tree of knowledge of good and evil (Genesis 2:16–17) became fact: physical death, distorted human personality, corrupted relationships, and alienation from God (Ephesians 2:1–3; Romans 3:10–18, 23). Paul's comment about humankind's enslavement to "elementary principles of the world" (Galatians 4:13) perhaps summarizes the effect of the Fall and accounts for human self-centered thinking. Eve would experience pain and difficulty in childbirth; Adam remained responsible to work the soil, but now with toil and effort, as if creation was directly opposing his efforts.

Adam and Eve's free will and choice to disobey God led to the sin and evil which surrounds us in our world. The consequences of the action of our "first father and mother," including disease and disability, passed on to all humankind. Humankind remains morally accountable to God, who generally allows us to experience the consequences of our choices and actions. Much of the suffering we experience is a result of our own sinfulness and poor choices, or decisions made "against us" by others (e.g., violence or cruelty). Just as the ground no longer produces its fruits without labor and difficulty, our ability to choose good over evil is hindered by our sin-nature. Our will is not totally free but is bound by sin, and God has abandoned humankind in the lusts of our hearts to impurity, dishonorable passions, and debased minds, which result in acts of idolatry, immorality, and self-centered indulgence (Romans 1:21–32). The free will explanation accounts for moral evil (inhumanity and cruelty) and partly explains some of the "natural evil" that results from misuse of God's creation (such as deforestation that leaves land barren, or pollution).

Answering the Problem: Natural Order

Related to the argument of the free-will defense, is the concept of natural order. In this view, suffering is the consequence, or logical result of natural events; moral issues are not necessarily involved. Disease, disruptions in nature (storms, floods, droughts, etc.) are the logical consequence of living in a fallen world—a world that "groans' while it eagerly awaits future glory which will transcend the hardships, pain, and affliction of the present (Romans 8:18–19). Genetic abnormalities, birth complications, and accidents, therefore, can be generally attributed to the fallen nature of humankind. They are the logical result of the original moral choice of Adam and Eve and the consequent curse on the ground (representing all creation), bringing "chaos' rather than the order with which God initially created the world. God generally does not interfere with these events, but allows them to run their natural course. God's not temporarily suspending the natural laws he embedded in creation makes for stability in our experience, a stability that would be absent were God to constantly intervene. If God stepped in to alter the outcome of a natural event for one person, that might at the same time create more difficulty for someone else, and could present a picture of God as acting arbitrarily. Hence, if I trip, I fall. God does not suspend the law of gravity in order to prevent me from being injured or disabled as a result of the fall. God *could* intervene, but he generally does not. Again, personal sin is not always at play. Jesus emphasized this in Luke 13:4–5 when asking if the 18 persons who were killed when the tower in Siloam fell were worse offenders that others living in Jerusalem. The implication is that they died, not because of their sin, but because of their proximity to the tower when it collapsed. Jesus performed many miracles—curing people of diseases or disabilities, even restoring life to some. But these miracles were to prove his deity and to demonstrate that a time of restoration had begun with his ministry. Whether Adam ever dropped a coconut on his toe or needed Eve to massage his aching back *prior* to Genesis 3 is not something we can answer with confidence, but certainly *after* the Fall this was the case given the changed natural order that resulted from their disobedience. I think we can safely assume that hurricanes, tornadoes, and earthquakes are a sign of creation's groaning, and disabilities that people may experience as a result of these events are simply logical consequences of the way the world "works."

Answering the Problem: Spiritual Warfare

Another explanation for suffering, pain, and disability connects directly to the free-will argument. Adam and Eve's disobedience is tied to the temptation of Satan, who is God's enemy. Isaiah 14:12–16 and Ezekiel 28:11–19 are understood to be descriptions of Satan's fall from his high position as, perhaps, "prime angel" before God. Though full of wisdom, perfect in beauty, and originally blameless in all his ways, the sin of pride corrupted his thinking and he sought to usurp God's position as the Most High. He wanted not just to be "like" God, but to *become*

God. God, of course, threw him out of heaven. Imagine Satan's anger—first at being cast down, but then to watch as God created humans *in God's image*—something which Satan wanted so desperately. Hence, there is spiritual warfare that will continue until the day the Lord acts to destroy evil altogether. We see the effects of this spiritual warfare in individual lives, families, cultures, and even sometimes in the church.

While not denying personal responsibility for sinful choices we make, nor suggesting that everything bad or unwanted that happens in our lives is the work of Satan or his demonic forces, we do recognize that "the God of this age" (2 Corinthians 4:4) is the instigator of much of the misery and turmoil seen in the world today. In fact, this turmoil gives Satan pleasure, since his goal is to disrupt God's plan and to prevent people from believing in and worshiping God. Not being equal to God, however, Satan cannot act without God's permission (cf. Job 1:9). We take comfort, thus, in knowing that what Satan does is not outside of God's eternal plan and purpose and control. God is sovereign over Satan's demonic forces, his hand in persecution, his life-harming or life-taking power, his hand in natural disasters, his sickness-causing power, and his spiritual bondage. Though Satan's intent is to steal our minds and bodies, to kill our soul, and to destroy our spirit and our hope, Jesus's purpose is to give us a full and satisfying life (John 10:10).

Answering the Problem: Greater Good

The greater good defense offers an explanation as to why God permits evil. It reasons that God allows evil in order to bring about something greater, something good. Although we sin freely, God can use sinful acts to bring blessing to many. Certainly, God does not like sin, suffering, or evil, but he allows it because of the greater good it can bring to the lives of people. For example, God might bring "good" through a disabled person's life that, when seen in the larger scope or context, outweighs the limitation of the disability. This could include bringing glory to himself through the life-witness of the person who is disabled, or using that person to bring others the good news of grace and restoration and hope through Christ (such as Joni Eareckson Tada). God brought much glory to himself, and drew many into the family of Christ, through the evil act of men in torturing and crucifying Jesus Christ. God has the ability and the wisdom to bring the greatest good out of what we perceive as bad.

This is what enabled Paul to write, "we know that for those who love God all things work together for good, for those who are called according to his purpose" (Romans 8:28) and to boast in his weakness so that the power of Christ would rest on him (2 Corinthians 11:30, 12:9). Essentially, this view asserts that God can (or will) bring about a greater good through what we perceive as evil, and maintains that the amount of good in the world outweighs (or will outweigh) the amount of evil in the world.

Responding to the Correct Question

Each of these explanations for the presence of evil and suffering contains truth. They are not contradictory, but complimentary in helping us to understand the world in which we live. But it is important to remember that God's ways are not our ways (Isaiah 55:8–9) and that the Lord is righteous in all that he does (Psalm 145:17). These answers primarily address the theological or philosophical side of the problem. For an individual or family dealing with disability, who are more focused on a specific situation, these arguments may seem unsatisfying or simply lead to further questions. Even if the person is able to accept the logic in these arguments, they may bring little comfort. When counseling someone facing disability-related issues, it is helpful to distinguish between the *problem of evil* (an intellectual and academic concern) and the *problem of suffering* (an existential and practical issue). A proper pastoral response requires knowing which issue the person faces: The problem of *evil* is an intellectual question requiring an intellectual answer. The problem of *suffering*, however, is a practical question focusing on everyday matters of coping and resolution. We must discern which question is being asked and respond accordingly: Intellectual answers to practical questions may seem hollow; practical responses to intellectual questions may seem shallow (Clark & Emmett, 1998). Ravi Zacharias related this story that illustrates my point:

> I remember in the early years of my ministry when I was being asked by a couple why God allows suffering in our lives. I sat facing them as they remained in the last pew of the church after everyone had gone. As I leaned forward to respond to their question I suddenly noticed their baby lying beside them, obviously born with Down's syndrome. I mentally stepped back for a moment, I knew then that their question struck deep into the heart. This was not an academic question. Their feelings were real, and so my answer needed to be. (1998, p. 71).

Several common misconceptions need to be avoided in our own and other's thinking about disability. One, which I have already addressed, is that disability or suffering represents God's judgment on personal sin. This was the assumption of Job's "counselors" and the thought underlying the disciples's question about the man who was born blind (John 9). The biggest problem with this misconception is that *all* have sinned and fall short of the glory of God (Romans 3:23). Why, then, are only some people disabled? It is not that someone is a greater sinner than another; God does not see "levels" of sin. Sin is sin, and the same judgment of God falls upon all who sin (cf. James 2:10)

A second misconception is that God is intentionally trying to teach the sufferer a lesson. Some might refer to Genesis 22 where God tested Abraham's faith by asking him to sacrifice Isaac on the altar. Though God used this as a means of deepening Abraham's faith and character, it is *not* to be understood as a normative experience for all believers. And in any case, God intervened to stop Abraham from sacrificing Isaac. The difficulty with this misconception is twofold: it places us in a position of judging God's actions (by our standards, not his), and it makes God's dealings with humankind arbitrary, stressing his sovereignty at the expense of his love.

Some have claimed that God especially loves a person who has a child with a disability. They suggest that disabled children are "sent" only to special parents. But this seems to be negated by the fact that having a child with severe or multiple disabilities can add significant stress into the family, possibly even disrupting the unity of the family as one parent may emotionally separate from the spouse or child. And, according to a study by Sullivan and Knutson (2000), child abuse and neglect is experienced at a rate three times that of children without disabilities. In addition, the suggestion that God might purposely disable a child in order to "bless" the parents devalues the child.

A related misconception is that disabilities are a special blessing, an affliction allowed by God as a sign of his special grace or love. The "logic" behind this view is possibly drawn from the biblical stories of Joseph (who rose to greatness in Egypt) and Job (who was restored to health, regained wealth, and gained a second family). However, the history of these two men does not provide a model or picture of God's normal way of operating. There are far more instances where a person's or a family's suffering has *not* been rewarded (at least in this life) as were Joseph and Job.

One very dangerous teaching is that of a "health and prosperity gospel." This teaching maintains that Christians ought to be immune from evil and suffering, often using a misinterpretation of Jeremiah 29:11 to support the claim. For someone not to prosper or to become disabled, is thought to be a sign of lack of faith, or that the person has unconfessed sin or is suffering the consequences of parental sin. Jeremiah 29:11 speaks of God's plans to "prosper" actually refers to *peace* (shalom). Specifically it speaks to the promised return of the Jews from exile. The biggest problem presented by this misconception/misinterpretation is that it denies the reality of suffering among God's people as well as denying the universality of moral and natural evil. Nowhere in the Bible does God promise every believer that, in this life, they will or should experience only health and material prosperity.

What is a Proper Pastoral Response to People Dealing with Disability?

Offering a purely theological or philosophical explanation as to why evil and suffering or disability exist, no matter how biblically accurate the explanation is, will mean little to the individual and family dealing with disability. A proper pastoral approach is to provide whatever support we can to ease the emotional and spiritual anguish the person or family may be experiencing. "We don't love others in the midst of this kind of pain by pretending that it isn't all that bad or by trying to quickly fix it with some pat theological answers" (Shramek, 2006, p. 177). At first, an appropriate response may simply be to sit with them and listen both to their words and the emotion that lies beneath. We may even need to cry with them, entering into their pain even though we cannot fully relate to their experience. Our presence is critical, since they may believe no one will accept them because of the disability. Our approach should be modeled after Jesus's, who identified with humanity in every way, including suffering and disability. In John 11:32, we are told that Mary, grieving the death of her brother, Lazarus, went quickly to where Jesus was. When Jesus saw her weeping, he was "deeply moved in his spirit and greatly troubled" (John 11:33). In the same way that Jesus identified with the grief of Mary and Martha, we should identify with the sorrow of those who face disability issues—indeed, with the suffering of all who are oppressed or cast aside. The deep anger that welled up within Jesus was directed toward sin and its effect (sickness, disability, death, etc). We also should be angry about how sin has corrupted creation, but *not* angry with the individual because of supposed unconfessed sin that brought about the disability.

There are actually three issues related to evil and suffering of any kind, all of which should provide guidance for pastoral care of individuals and families affected by disability. The first is obvious: the problem itself (e.g., becoming disabled and all that this entails; the birth of a child with disabilities). The second issue is the spiritual challenge this presents (Where is God? Have I sinned?). The third issue is how other people—both churched and unchurched—respond to the individual or family. Unhelpful responses include those which show misunderstanding of the person's experience and of disability; offer unhelpful advice (like Job's counselors); make light of the problem ("it's not that bad"); or fail to show an effort to identify with the person. These responses produce *relational* and *psychological* problems which result in isolation and compound the situation. A proper response will bring comfort to the person (2 Corinthians 1:4), which brings encouragement and hope to the person. It is to provide what Powlison (2006) called "God's transformative compassion, the perfect union of kindness and candor" (p. 166). It is drawing from how God brought comfort in our difficulties and being helpful to others in *any* situation.

Where is God when People Suffer?

Evil is a mystery rather than a problem (Kreeft, 1986, p. 50)—problems are solvable; mysteries are not. If God has no control over evil, then evil is senseless and it is meaningless to ask "Why is there suffering?" To ask this question assumes the existence of God and assumes that suffering does have meaning.

Our difficulty is that our understanding is limited. As stated earlier, the Bible teaches that God's ways (purposes) are mysterious (Isaiah 55:8–9). They are far beyond our ability to comprehend. Our human tendency is to focus on the *present* rather than the future. But a future orientation, which recognizes the temporariness of this world, is more appropriate to the Christian life. In anticipation of eternal blessing, the Bible urges contentment rather than "happiness" as it is commonly understood (cf. Philippians 4:11–12; Hebrews 13:5).

Living a victorious Christian life does not require that our bodies be "whole," only that our heart be right with God. Restoration and reconciliation are what is important, but these come through God's grace, not our ability. A "cure" for disability is not what is needed; but healing of our spirit and soul is necessary.

Even though people naturally seek an answer to the question "Why?" in relation to becoming disabled or birthing a child who is disabled, the ultimate answer is often never received. God never explained to Job why he suffered as he did. Instead, God reminded Job of who he is as the Creator and Sovereign. Ultimately, we must rest in the knowledge of who God is, and trust his love and wisdom. Overly focusing on the issues of theodicy can distract us from the social elements that are at play, either in causing disability or as they impact the spiritual and social life of the person who is disabled. Social elements which are often correlates of disability—poverty, malnutrition, unavailability of basic medical care, rampant social injustice, and the like—are things which we, as individuals and as the Church of God can and should address.

Going Deeper

1. The reason God created the world was that God is inclined to display the fullness of his greatness for people to know, praise, and enjoy; in other words, out of passion for his glory (Piper, 1998). This includes creating a world in which disability was possible, although not *actual* until after the Fall. Being disabled does not prevent the fullness of God's glory from being displayed. As Paul wrote in 2 Corinthians 12, it is in our weakness that God's power and glory is manifest. Far from avoiding the problems of humanity, the good news of the Gospel promises that "out of weakness will come strength and out of sorrow will come comfort" (Russell, 2002). How does this change (or challenge) your view of disability and weakness?

2. How would you respond to the young parents of a baby born with Down's syndrome that Ravi Zacharias mentioned? What information do they need (if any, at this time)? How would you assure them of God's love—for them *and* for the baby? What hope can you give them? How can you and your church come along side this family?

Chapter Nine

Concluding Thoughts

The Gospels declare that Jesus went about proclaiming the good news of the kingdom (Luke 4:43, 8:1). He said the kingdom of God was "at hand" (Matthew 4:17, 10:7), had "come near" (Luke 10:9, 11:20), and was "in their midst" (Luke 17:21). The kingdom was present because the King was present. The word *kingdom* does not refer to a place, but to a realm in which a king exercises authority. God, of course, is always at work, shaping history to its designated end. But usually God works "behind the scenes" to accomplish his will. Rarely has God "visibly broken into time and space to set his unmistakable imprint on events" (Richards, 1999, p. 378). God did this at the Exodus, powerfully bringing his people out of captivity in Egypt, and again when the Son of God took on human form, and Jesus acted to break the power of sin and free his people from captivity to Satan. With Jesus came a demonstration of the power of God and a beginning to the destruction of the dominion of sin and Satan. Satan's dominion began to crumble when Jesus overcame the temptations in the wilderness (Matthew 4:1–11) and continued as Jesus cast out demons and cured many of disease and disability (Matthew 12:28; Luke 9:11, 11:20; Acts 10:38). This destruction culminated in the crucifixion and resurrection of Jesus, so that "death was swallowed up in victory" (1 Corinthians 15:54; Hebrews 2:14).

At the final judgment (Revelation 20:2, 10) the destruction of Satan's dominion will become fully evident, but in the meantime the battle continues. The Acts of the Apostles details the ongoing warfare as the Gospel message was carried throughout the known world. Paul related specific details about his particular struggles in his epistles. Though in the fullest sense, the battle is the Lord's, Christians today continue to engage in spiritual warfare. To assist in this continuing battle, God gave us the Holy Spirit (Luke 12:12; John 14:26), graced us with spiritual gifts (1 Corinthians 12:4–11), and provided us with his armor (Ephesians 6:11–18). This continuing battle is for the hearts and minds of people, to bring them into the kingdom. We fight against the influence of Satan and of culture, seeking to bring every thought captive to Christ (2 Corinthians 10:5). Paul urges that we set our minds on the things of the Spirit, which is life and peace (Romans 8:5–6).

Part of this battle involves rescuing people with disabilities from the lie that they are worthless, that their life is meaningless, that they are less than human. This requires working directly with people and families affected by disability: *evangelistically,* sharing Christ with them; *spiritually,* to give them hope in the Lord and help them discover the talents and gifts God has placed within them; *physically,* to nurture latent skills and abilities or to help them learn new skills; *materially,* to meet their needs as God enables us; and *relationally,* building community and allowing them to minister to others, including those who remain temporarily able-bodied.

We have noted that people seek predictability and safety in their world, a stability that orients them in life, sometimes taking extreme measures to insure security against anything perceived as a threat. This helps explain why people who are disabled may initially be suspicious of our intent and reject or be slow to respond to overtures of friendship from "outsiders" who are not disabled. The Church of Christ must be a place of safety and security for all people. Thus, our outreach must be done with patience and consistency, accepting the individual where he or she "is," but not content to leave them there. We model the love of Jesus by doing acts of kindness such as those described in Matthew 25:24–40, offering these acts as if ministering directly to Jesus, and without expectation of reward from those we minister to. Along with compassionate concern for those who suffer, the Church must seek to promote and establish justice for those who are oppressed. Our love is not an abstract feeling offered from a distance, but is action-based as we do what we can to create a God-centered community that offers salvation, health, physical care, nurturing, support, reconciliation—in biblical terms, *shalom*.

Being Christ in a Broken World

Being Christ in a broken world requires that we become Christlike in our character. Paul spoke of this transformation in Romans 12:1–2, where he urged renewal of our minds so that we are not conformed to the world's ideas and values. This transformation begins at the time of our redemption when, in Christ, we become a new creation (2 Corinthians 5:17). It means being completely surrendered to God, to whom we belong by creation and redemption—not patterning ourselves after the world but being entirely renovated in thinking and behavior, refusing the norms of conduct and thought employed by the world whenever and wherever they are not in accord with God's revealed will and proscribed patterns of behavior. This transformation does not happen overnight, but is an ongoing process of continual renewal and transformation as we continually offer ourselves to God and we are molded more and more into the image of Christ.

Four aspects of Christlikeness especially relate to disability ministry: *incarnation, vulnerability, servanthood,* and *justice.* To be "incarnate" requires that we remain open to interacting with people who are disabled—being accepting and welcoming, rather than fearful and distant. As Jesus broke through many barriers in his ministry, we must also be willing to dismantle any barriers that prevent the gospel from being shared with individuals who are disabled, and willing to challenge society and culture to recognize the humanity and the needs of all peoples.

Being Christ in a broken world also calls us to recognize our own vulnerability, such as to being misunderstood or rejected, and our weaknesses and dependence on God and others. Paul's analogy between the human body and the church (1 Corinthians 12:12–26) clearly show our need for one another. Paul argued that those parts of the body which appear to be weaker or of lesser importance are actually indispensable (12:22). Though seemingly weaker and less visible, these individuals still have God-given gifts which make them essential to the functioning of the body. Fritzen (2004) claimed that this verse is Paul's way of saying "we cannot discover our strength without acknowledging our weakness" (p. 12). In truth, we must admit that whatever is accomplished in our ministry is really God's working through our weakness—something God wants much more than our strength (cf. 2 Corinthians 12:9–10).

To be Christ in a broken world demands that we have the same attitude toward service as Jesus (Philippians 2:3–8), who came not to be served but to serve. A prime illustration of Jesus's humility and servanthood was his washing the feet of his disciples and instructing them to follow his example of humility and servanthood (John 13:1–16).

And to be Christ in a broken world means that his concern for justice for people who have been marginalized and oppressed must be maintained in our ministry, recognizing that justice and peace are concerns of the Gospel (Anderson, 1985). We do call people to repentance and to accept Christ as their personal Savior, but, just as God's prophets did in the past, we must also address social, institutionalized sin that keeps people in bondage—e.g., poverty, prostitution, disease, prejudice, and all forms of injustice. Like God's prophets, and like Christ himself, we must speak for those who cannot speak for themselves (Proverbs 31:8–9). Being Christ in a broken world means that we must have a passion to reach people who are spiritually lost, who are in bondage in any way. Wiersbe's (2001b) comment is relevant: "The way we behave toward people indicates what we really believe about God!"

Inclusion

Inclusion of students with disabilities in school programs is a current emphasis in many countries around the world. But inclusion in a broader sense is about developing societies that embrace diversity (Naicker, 2003). Arora (2009) stated, "If we are to be like God, if we are to be in community with God, we too must join the struggle for access and inclusion with regard to all of God's people" (p. 30). For this to occur, there is a continuing need to promote understanding of the humanity and the abilities of persons with disabilities so that rather than being "written off" and forgotten, they are empowered to function effectively as contributing members of society. The negative societal attitudes toward persons with disabilities described earlier in this book, however, suggest that citizens with disabilities continue to be unnoticed and unserved or under-served despite official (governmental) proclamations to the contrary. The Church finds its true identity when it fully integrates itself with people who are marginalized: the diseased and disabled, widows and orphans, and other who are rejected or oppressed (Otieno, 2009).

Attempting to address this problem using a top-down (legislative) approach is likely to have little impact. Efforts to promote services for persons with disabilities which build from the concept of community-based rehabilitation seem to hold greater promise. The intent is to work within the person's home area to promote participation in all aspects of community life. Community-based rehabilitation creates a linkage between persons with disabilities, non governmental organizations, and key members of the community (professionals and agencies). To have a real impact on the culture and society, the Church needs to become an essential player in promoting and providing community acceptance and provision of necessary services.

Role of the Church

In many countries, the largest group which can serve and advocate for persons with disabilities and their families, other than the government, is the Christian Church. And the Church can do it better since it operates in the Spirit and power of the Lord. Churches and church-related schools are appropriate places to initiate socio-cultural change within developing nations. Biblical

Christianity clearly teaches that human worth and dignity—and consequently human rights—are not dependent on "wholeness" or being able-bodied. The Christian community needs to be awakened and mobilized so that it can take a leadership role in meeting the needs of persons with disabilities in both churches and society. Churches and para-church organizations can impact the lives of significant numbers of people in developing nations by promoting understanding of disabling conditions (their cause, prevention, and treatment), integrating persons with disabilities into the Christian community and society as a whole, and recognizing the basic rights of such persons. This should begin with theological colleges and seminaries which prepare church leaders who, in turn, will encourage within their congregations acceptance and valuing of all people.

The role of the Church should be to create communities in which people who are not alike can be found living and working together (McCollum, 1998). In doing this, the Church will take its rightful position in shaping culture, and will be a visible expression of God's love for all humanity through constructive protest against the present conditions of men and women with disabilities. The Church must be concerned about social justice for persons who are disabled, and not relinquish this role to the government or to secular social agencies.

Churches should lead the way in seeking to establish reconciled and reconciling communities which not only work toward restoration of right relationships between God and humankind, but also toward right relationships between individuals—all genders, all races, all cultures, all social strata, and all ability levels. Ministering to and with persons who have a disability necessitates a proactive approach by Kingdom people, with the same compelling spirit Paul spoke of in 2 Corinthians 5:14, and the same urgency with which the servant was sent out to compel the poor, crippled, blind, and lame to come to the great banquet (Luke 14:21).

The gospel is about transformation, transformation of every aspect of creation. The Bible clearly asserts the Lordship of Jesus over the forces and divisions which bring enmity between people (Ephesians 2:11–18). Hence, the Church should engage the culture, bringing to bear on culture and social issues God's transforming truth and the presence of Jesus. The Church must lead in the movement away from ignorance, insensitivity, and indifference toward acceptance and reconciliation, actively seeking to remove barriers which exclude disabled persons from all aspects of society. This must be done wisely and openly—acknowledging that the Church and the culture are equally guilty of having neglected the disabled, and confessing its sin of omission and exclusion. If the Church is truly to have an incarnational presence in the world, it must be more open in welcoming and championing equal rights on behalf of persons with disabilities. There can be no escaping Jesus's example and teaching in the parables about reaching out to "the least of these" (Matthew 25) and of including in the gospel invitation those whom society (religious and civil) has tended to reject (cf. Luke 14:15–24).

The Church of Christ must go beyond humanitarian objectives alone to minister holistically, addressing spiritual and relational needs as well as physical and social needs (cf. Fuller, 1987). For the Church to be salt and light in society (Matthew 5:13–14) necessitates speaking out against any form of discrimination and injustice, especially against those who cannot defend themselves. The Church must advocate for and defend the welfare and human rights of even the most severely disabled, recognizing that all people are God's children by creation and have equal value as God's image bearers. God does not exclude people on the basis of ability; neither can the Church.

The Church must be a change agent in society through living a lifestyle of reconciliation and acceptance. Jesus's focus on including the excluded must be that of all Christians.

The life of Christ flows through Christians to others. Our service is Jesus acting through us to bring blessing, comfort, and life to those we minister to and with. This book began with a reference to Matthew 9:35–38, which spoke of Jesus's great compassion for people who are "like sheep without a shepherd." Jesus encouraged his followers to pray to the Lord of the harvest that workers be sent into the fields to bring in the harvest. We are those workers. The life of Christ has been given to us to serve others, not just to make us righteous. "We are given the compassion of Christ so that we will be compassionate" (Walker, 2010, p. 189). Jesus's life, love, care, and strength flow through us to others, and the glory goes to him.

The Advantage of Disability

Physical brokenness is a reminder of human finiteness and that the world is vastly different from what God originally intended (Beates, 2012). Disability, as part of that brokenness, is a tool God can use to bring people to him. Disability, in ourselves or someone in our family, helps free us from trusting in our "power" and "ability." In 1 Corinthians 1:27–29, Paul said God has chosen what is weak and foolish, low and despised, in the eyes of the world to shame the wise and strong, so that we would have nothing to boast of in the presence of God. Temporarily able-bodied persons often think that people who are disabled are weak and foolish, with nothing to offer, but the Bible's teaching places us all in the category of weak and foolish. Paul also described us as jars of clay, like broken pots into which God has placed the treasure of the Gospel (2 Corinthians 4:7) to show that God's power is operative, not our own. God "chooses and uses those the world least expects to achieve his ends and to bring glory to himself" (Beates, 2012, p. 63).

Mike Cope, father of a child with a mental disability, provided a illustration of God's irony in using what the world considers weak to teach others, by sharing what he learned from his daughter:

> She taught me that God will use my brokenness to his glory. She reminded me that the power is God's, not mine. She made me remember that we are often fascinated with things that are impressive from the outside but which may not be that important to God. She taught me that what really matters has to do with the heart: keeping promises, seeking justice in a brutal world, learning to see those in greatest need, and living with courage, joy, and unconditional love. (Cope, 2011, p. 29)

We might say, therefore, that people with disabilities have a advantage over the temporarily able-bodied: they know their limitations and weaknesses. Jesus's great compassion for the poor, widows, orphans, and oppressed evidences that they are close to the heart of God. People with disabilities can help able-bodied people recognize their own need for grace from the Lord, their own "poverty" and dependence. Nouwen spoke of his learning of the "gift of the handicapped" through his work with severely disabled persons:

> They see through a facade of smiles and friendly words and sense the resentful heart before we ourselves notice it. Often they are capable of unmasking our impatience,

irritation, jealousy, and lack of interest and making us honest with ourselves. For them, what really counts is a true relationship, a real friendship, a faithful presence . . . . Their heart registers with extreme sensitivity what is real care and what is false, what is true affection and what is just empty words. Thus, they often reveal to us our own hypocrisies and invite us always to greater sincerity and purer love. (Nouwen, 1988, p. 19)

We could even say that persons who are disabled help the able-bodied to become more human.

Going Deeper

1. How can you, or your church, engage in community-based rehabilitation? What services or NGOs already exists in your community that you can connect with—or that you can help people with disabilities connect with? If you are unaware of these kinds of contacts, how can you go about finding them?

2. What would it take for you or your church to be able to collaborate with other churches or secular organizations to serve people with disabilities and their families?

3. Do you agree or disagree with Otieno's statement that the Church finds its true identity when it fully integrates itself with people who are marginalized? With respect to people with disabilities, what is *your* church's identity? How would a person with a disability describe your church?

4. Otieno (2009) went on to say that a major cause of discriminatory acts against persons with disabilities is religion-related. She argued that theological interpretations of disability have shaped society's view of these individuals, and biblical texts have often been interpreted in oppressive ways. This has contributed to the marginalization and exclusion of disabled persons in various arenas of society, including the church. How can you help others in your church develop more appropriate (godly) attitudes toward people who face issues of disability?

5. We read in John 12:44–46 these words of Jesus: "Whoever believes in me, believes not in me but in him who sent me. And whoever sees me sees him who sent me. I have come into the world as light, so that whoever believes in me may not remain in darkness." Christians are re-presentations of Jesus, we act as his hands and feet and voice in the world today. Do people who see you, see the One who sent you? Do you shine as a light, especially towards individuals and families affected by disability?

6. Are you and your church a visible expression of God's love for *all* people?

Section Four

Going Deeper into God's Word

For Your Continued Study

Amos Yong (2011) has written a useful book to present Scripture from the viewpoint of disability. In *The Bible, Disability, and the Church*, Yong invites his readers to "revisit the scriptural material in order to rethink disability in our time" (p. 6). He explains that able-bodied people tend to have a "normate" bias against people with disabilities. A *normate* bias is essentially an unquestioned worldview that reinforces the idea that people with disabilities are less than normal. He acknowledges that much of the Bible has been read and understood in a way that supports this view and has attempted to counter the *normate* perspective through this, and his previous book on *Theology and Down Syndrome* (2007).

Yong's position corresponds to what I have developed in this book. He asserts that people with disabilities are created in the image of God, and that all people face various challenges and have weaknesses. His position is that difficulties faced by people with disabilities have been intensified by the *normate* bias of non disabled people. He argues that the disability should not be seen as the defining factor of a person, adding that people with disabilities are generally able to determine their own needs and desires and should not be regarded as helpless. Disabilities are not necessarily evil or nor are they blemishes that must be eliminated (2011, p. 13).

A *normate* perspective suggests that to be a disciple of Jesus requires a "whole" body, or one that is restored to "wholeness" through cure. This creates a negative view of disability and people who are disabled. Yong explores several key biblical passages to help readers reconsider what is being taught so that they are not seen to reflect a biblical bias against disability or disabled persons. He points out that the Gospels place less stress on bodily cure than on the saving power of Christ and concludes, "The saving work of God can occur even if the curing of bodies doesn't happen, and we would do well to assure people with disabilities that cures are not the norm by which to measure the reality of divine salvation" (2011, p. 66). Yong's book is essential reading for people wishing to engage the Christian culture regarding the need for reaching out to people with disabilities and bringing them fully into the Church family to live, love, and serve along with those who are able-bodied.

* * * * * * *

The short Bible studies which follow are designed to help you dig deeper into God's Word and issues of disability. Many of the Scripture portions selected for study will be familiar. My interest is in getting you to think of how they might relate to disability and disability ministry—to look at them through a disability lens. The questions ask you to stretch you thinking beyond the typical application of these passages. I find it difficult to read passages from the Bible and *not* see some way they can be related to disability ministry. Hopefully, as you have worked your way through this book, you have become more attuned to this and will be less inclined to read the Bible with a *normate* bias.

Through the Roof: Mark 2:1–12

Mark 2:1–12 is a familiar passage to many, but its familiarity may lead to missing some insights that relate to ministry to and with persons who are disabled and their families. Read the passage carefully and be open to new ideas about ministry as you consider the following thoughts and questions.

1. Obviously there was a prior relationship between the man who was paralyzed and the four men who brought him to Jesus. Were they relatives? Where they friends? If his paralysis was from an accident, might they have been co-workers concerned for their colleague?

2. The men took it upon themselves to bring the man who was paralyzed to Jesus—there is no indication that he had asked them to do this. What do you think led them to take this action? They did not allow the situation (crowds preventing them from getting to Jesus) to deter them. No obstacle was going to keep them from accomplishing their task, not even if it meant removing part of the roof to lower the man to Jesus. What do you learn from this about what your attitude should be in ministering to and with people who are disabled?

3. Would the man who was paralyzed ever have met Jesus were it not for these four men? Note that it was *their* faith that led not only to the man being cured of his disability but also to his receiving forgiveness for his sin. Would you go out of your way to help someone with a disability to "meet" Jesus?

4. How can you follow the example of these four men and seek to "bring" people with disabilities to Jesus?

5. By first forgiving the man of sin, Jesus was *not* indicating that his sin had caused his disability. Why did Jesus grant him forgiveness before curing him of his paralysis? For whose benefit (other than the paralyzed man) did Jesus perform the miracle of curing his disability?

6. How did Jesus's response to the man differ from that of the scribes who were present? They were not wrong in saying "Who can forgive sin but God alone." The tone of their question implies condemnation of Jesus. Why were they so quick to judge him for his words? What did they not understand about Jesus?

7. What do you think would have been the response of the scribes and other leaders of the Jews if the four men had brought their paralyzed friend to them seeking help?

8. Put yourself in the place of the man who was paralyzed. How would your life be different if you were paralyzed? What would be your response *after* having your sins forgiven—and *after* you were cured? Do you think he slowly and quietly walked home after leaving Jesus's presence?

9. Which *is* easier to say: "Your sins are forgiven" or "Get up and walk"?

Jesus Cures a Man of Leprosy: Luke 5:12–14

Read Luke 5:12–14, a record of Jesus's encounter with a man with leprosy. "Leprosy" was a term used for several infectious skin diseases, including Hansen's disease. You may want to look at Leviticus 13 and 14 for background on the laws regarding leprosy. The Law said that people with leprosy were obliged to remain apart from others (Leviticus 13:46), which may have been worse than the disease itself. They were cut off from family and friends, who feared catching the disease, yet this man boldly approached Jesus.

1. What do you think led him to break the law and approach Jesus? Was it desperation? Did he just believe that Jesus might cure him, or did he know more of who Jesus was? Does it matter? Did Jesus only cure people who professed faith in him as Lord?

2. When the man with leprosy came to Jesus, Luke tells us he fell on his face before Jesus and said "Lord, if you will, you can make me clean." The man's action in pleading for help conveyed the emotional "pain" he experienced by being isolated and shunned by the community. What happens if the people of Christ push aside, step over, or go around people who are diseased or disabled? What does that tell people about Jesus?

3. Note what Jesus did in response to the man before he said "I will; be clean." Jesus stretched out his hand and touched the man. This action of Jesus is very informative to our ministry. He did not keep the man at a distance (which would mean Jesus also was distant). That the man was lying on the ground meant that Jesus had to stoop down in order to touch him, but there was no hesitation on Jesus's part. Why is it significant that Jesus reached down and *touched* him? What does it teach us about humility and service? What does it reveal about the depth of Jesus's compassion? What does this tell us about our approach to people with disabilities? How can you adopt similar attitudes in ministry to people who are diseased or disabled, and their families?

4. Jesus could simply have spoken and cured him, but Jesus *touched* the man. We do not know how long this man had been diseased and living apart from family and friends. This could have been his first physical contact from another human in many years. How do you think he felt when Jesus touched him? Jesus's touch may have been as important to the man's cure as his actual cleansing. Jesus's absence of fear or hesitation about physically touching the man provides a model for us in ministry with persons who are disabled. How ready do you feel to physically engage with a person who is disabled?

5. Note that Jesus instructed the man to follow what the Old Testament law required—to show himself to the priest (to be declared "clean") and present the requisite offering. Jesus not only cured him of his disease, but was restoring him to the religious community. What does this teach about the end-goal of ministry with people who are diseased (e.g., HIV/AIDS) or disabled today?

6. Some people link leprosy with sin (though it may be more correctly likened to death). But in this incidence of cure, there is no mention of the man's sin or the need for forgiveness. We must not make the mistake of thinking someone's being or becoming disabled is attributable to sin. And even if it was, isn't the proper Christian response compassion?

The Vineyard Workers: Matthew 20:1–16

Read the complete parable. The workers hired first were displeased that those hired at the end of the day received the same wages. Their complaint was not over *their* pay, but the fact that those who did less of the labor received the *same* pay. In their mind, this was an injustice. Their focus was on themselves, not on the others. In their opinion, to do less work should result in less pay.

1. Suppose we modify the parable to equate those hired first with temporarily able-bodied persons, and those hired last with persons who are disabled. The complainers might be thinking "we have contributed much but the disabled workers have contributed little, yet earned the same reward." This corresponds with the assumption that people with disabilities are unable (or less able) to "do" in the church—that is, to personally or financially contribute to the church's ministry. They feel that those who are disabled will only "take from" the church (time, money, other resources); therefore, they deserve less. How would you respond to this?

2. Some might complain that people with disabilities, especially severe disabilities, do not look "normal" (that is, they don't look like "us") and should not be welcomed—or at least should not be seated where they will be visible to all who come. They may even be concerned that if people with disabilities are openly visible, able-bodied people might not want to be a part of the church. Can you see how this translates to saying that persons who are disabled have little or no value? Does a Christian's value depend on what he or she can *do* or is their value inherent in their *being* (i.e., the image of God in which all humans are created)?

3. Is church a place to "do"? When we gather together, is it to "do church"? Do we get rewarded for coming to church? What *is* the church? Why do we gather together? Do we go to church to get something out of it, or to give something to God?

4. Since it is by God's grace that we have been accepted as his children (Ephesians 2:8–10), Church should be a place characterized by grace and acceptance. Webb-Mitchell (1994a) stated, "living in Christ means living a life where grace is never a bounty to be earned" (p. 38). God's gift of love is undeserved but freely given, and humbly received. Was there any sign of grace or humility on the part of those who were unhappy with the master's action in the parable? Was there anything that indicated gratitude for the day's employment?

5. The complainers viewed the master's actions as unfair, believing the pay given the last-hired workers to be more than they deserved. But the master (Jesus) had a higher, more mature definition of fairness: rather than meaning everyone gets what they deserve, it means everyone gets what they *need*. Since each set of workers needed the day's wages for survival, the master's grace provided it.

   a. What implications can you draw from this about how the church (believers) should respond to people with disabilities?

   b. Rather than receiving less because they may only be able to "do" less, is it possible that, because God emphasizes caring for the oppressed, people with disabilities might be deserving of *more* than the able-bodied?

The Lost Sheep: Luke 15:3–7

Luke tells us Jesus gave this parable in answer to the grumbling of the Pharisees and scribes about his having fellowship with "sinners." The plot is familiar: The shepherds have brought the sheep together at the end of the day. Spending his days and nights caring for the flock, the shepherd is not only responsible for the sheep but knows each of them in a way that is probably unfamiliar to today's herders. Knowing that one is missing, he leaves the 99 in the care of other shepherds and goes to find the one that is missing. Kistemaker (1980) explained that a sheep isolated from the flock becomes confused. Rather than try to find the others, a sheep that has become separated will simply lie down and wait for the shepherd. It would not move, even in response to the shepherd's call. Once found, the shepherd in Jesus's parable lifts it to his shoulders and carries it to where the flock is waiting. We are not told how long or how far afield the shepherd had to search before finding the missing sheep, but whatever the distance, carrying a sheep that may weigh 70 pounds, though tiring, was not something the shepherd regretted. Upon meeting with the others, he calls his friends and neighbors to join him in joyous celebration. Jesus concluded by saying, "Just so, I tell you, there will be more joy in heaven over one sinner who repents than over ninety-nine righteous persons who need no repentance."

Let's think of this parable is terms of disability ministry. Think of the Pharisees and scribes, the ones who complained about Jesus associating with "sinners," as *temporarily able-bodied*. The lost sheep corresponds to a *person who is disabled*, someone who might be defenseless against the exploitation of others. Some in the church may be like the first group and grumble about reaching out to people with disabilities, reasoning that they are not worth the trouble, or have nothing to offer.

1. In Jesus's parable, the shepherd is God, who reaches out to all. But in our scenario, who would the shepherd represent?

2. The shepherd was conscientious and caring. He knew his flock intimately, knew that one was missing, made sure that the 99 were safe, went to search for the missing sheep, and carried the sheep back to the fold. What suggestions can you gather from this about pastoral care for people with disabilities?

3. What are specific ways you and your church can "shepherd" people who are disabled?

4. When the lost sheep was found and returned to the flock, there was rejoicing. What should be our attitude when a person who is disabled, or a family that is affected by disability, come to the church? When they come to Christ?

5. Jesus said there is more rejoicing over one who repents than over the other 99. Does that suggest God could be more pleased with the one disabled person than the 99 able-bodied?

6. Eugene (1999) observed that the church is often more concerned with the 99 members who are not disabled. But individuals with disabilities are "the people of the Gospels" (p. 23) and present the church with opportunity to give witness to the values of Jesus as expressed in his ministry. How can you proclaim the good news of the Gospel in a way that shows its relevance to the lives of people dealing with disability?

Mephibosheth: 2 Samuel 9:1–13

Mephibosheth is a relatively minor character in the story of David's rise to become King of Israel. Mephibosheth was the son of Jonathan, grandson of King Saul. Long before David became king, he and Jonathan has entered into a solemn covenant (1 Samuel 20:12–17, 42) in which David promised to faithfully show kindness to Jonathan's family should he be killed in battle.

2 Samuel 4:4 gives some background about Mephibosheth. We are told he became disabled at the age of five when word came that Saul and Jonathan had been killed. Fearing the enemy would seek to kill all of Saul's family, Mephibosheth's nurse fled with the child, but in her haste dropped him, injuring his legs in such a way that he became lame—an impairment or loss of the ability to walk because of rigidity or deformity. His disability made him unfit it the eyes of the culture to occupy the throne as Saul's one remaining descendant.

Possibly David was unaware of Mephibosheth. It had been several years since David and Jonathan made their covenant. By the time Mephibosheth is brought to David, he is a young man with a son of his own (2 Samuel 9:12). Typically, when someone new took over the throne, any relatives of the former ruler would be eliminated to prevent an attempt to retake power by the family. Very likely, this is what Mephibosheth anticipated when he was summoned before the King.

Carefully read the passage, and reflect on these questions:

1. David neither sought to eliminate Mephibosheth nor to show pity because of his disability. What was David's motivation to meet with Mephibosheth? What does that suggest should be our focus in reaching out to people who are disabled?

2. David transformed Mephibosheth from a helpless disabled person to a man of wealth and status. Saul's estate was restored to him, Ziba was appointed to oversee the estate on behalf of Mephibosheth, and Mephibosheth was made a member of David's household—"adopted" as a son to dine at the king's table. Note that David intentionally reached out to Mephibosheth. He did not hesitate to show kindness nor did his view of Mephibosheth change when he learned of his disability.

    a. How can you model that same grace and kindness to people with disabilities?

    b. What specific acts of kindness can you and your church do for individuals or families affected by disability?

    c. How can you and your church "find" people with disabilities in your community?

3. David's compassion for Mephibosheth was costly. How much are you willing to "spend" to demonstrate godly compassion on people who are disabled?

4. What was Mephibosheth's reaction to David's kindness (2 Samuel 9:8)? Do you think his referring to himself as a "dead dog" was simply self-degrading language to show deference or to grovel before the king? Or could this be a reflection of how he saw himself based on the culture's perspective of disability? What difference do you think David's kindness made in Mephibosheth's life?

Jacob—Disabled by God: Genesis 32:24–32

Jacob, son of Isaac and grandson of Abraham, is recognized as one of the major patriarchs in Israel's history. We know him as the father of 12 sons, from whom the tribes of Israel descended. Jacob's life story does not present him in the best light, however. His name means "deceiver," which seems an appropriate description of him as he managed to secure the birthright from his brother, and deceived his elderly and blind father into giving him the paternal blessing that would have gone to Esau. Of course, Jacob was not alone in this trickery; his mother, Rebekah, instigated Jacob's deception. Their duplicity, however, brought about what God had revealed even before the twins were born: the elder shall serve the younger (Genesis 25:23). Jacob fled from home after he received the blessing from his father, knowing the anger of Esau. By the time we reach Genesis 32, about 20 years have passed and Jacob is returning home with his family, servants, and livestock. He received word that Esau was coming to meet him and, concerned for the safety of his family, Jacob sent them to a safe location and was alone as night fell.

During the night, Jacob was visited by a "man" who wrestled with Jacob until dawn. Jacob appeared to be prevailing, until the visitor dislocated Jacob's hip, leaving him with a permanent disability. Despite being seriously injured, Jacob was able to cling to his opponent, and said he would not release his grip until he was blessed. Jacob was given a new name, *Israel*, meaning "he who strives with God." Jacob ultimately lost the match, but won a victory. God's gift of a disability helped him understand that his focus on himself and doing things his way was wrong, and to recognize his dependence upon God. Realizing it was God he struggled with, Jacob said "I have seen God face to face, yet my life has been spared" (Genesis 32:30, NLT).

Through the blessing of disability Jacob realized he could not overcome his opponent. His new name signified a changed life—no longer was he the "schemer and deceiver." The fullness of God's blessing included permanent disability, which would be a continual reminder of God's grace. As you meditate on this passage, consider these thoughts and questions:

1. That Jacob's becoming disabled was an act of God's grace is another way of describing the advantage of disability. His disability made it impossible for him to escape the reality of who he had been as Jacob, of God's mercy to him, and of who he became as Israel. Can you see the blessing of God in disabling Jacob?

2. Jacob's experience and blessing of disability somewhat parallels Paul's experience of God's refusal to remove his "thorn in the flesh" (2 Corinthians 12:7–10). Both men came to understand God's truth: "My grace is sufficient for you, for my power is made perfect in weakness" (2 Corinthians 12:9). How does this affect your view of disability and weakness? Can you see how God values our weakness more than our strength?

3. Suppose you have a good relationship with a family or an individual who is affected by disability. How could you use the story of Jacob's blessing of disability to encourage your friend? Would you be able to help them understand that it is possible for spiritual blessing and physical affliction to compliment one another and draw a person closer to God?

Greatest in the Kingdom: Matthew 18:1–6

This passage is part of a larger section in which Jesus teaches about relationships in the kingdom of God, and living a lifestyle consistent with God's kingdom, characterized by commitment to servanthood. The question the disciples really asked is "Which *of us* is the greatest in the kingdom of heaven?" They were preoccupied with the *organization* of the kingdom and what their position or status would be. Jesus responded by having a young child stand in their midst, probably directly in front of him and perhaps gently resting his hands on the child's shoulders. By his action and his teaching, Jesus refocused the question from *being greatest* to *entering* the kingdom: They must change and become like a child to give evidence of kingdom life. "Becoming like" a child was explained by Jesus as demonstrating humility.

In this way, Jesus exposed the spiritual immaturity of the disciples. He contrasted their ambition and the "littleness" (humbleness) of a child. Children—especially boys—were viewed as signs of God's blessing. But children were marginal members of society, with no legal standing or power. They were totally dependent on the good will of their parents, and generally regarded as insignificant. Making a child the center of attention probably startled and amazed the disciples.

On the surface, Jesus seems to be teaching and modeling respect and affirmation of young children, but to stop there is to miss Jesus's point. At the center of kingdom life are those who come to Christ with the openness, sincerity, trust, dependence, and vulnerability of little children. Jesus's action and teaching contrast with the culture's views of importance. In Jesus's pronouncement, he is talking about the character of *anyone* who enters the kingdom of God. His lesson is not about children, but about *kingdom values*. The child represents a "people-group" characterized by qualities or characteristics of humility, of "littleness."

1. The people-group represented by the little child would surely include people with disabilities. The disciples would be just as surprised if Jesus had used a disabled person as his example. What do think the disciples thought when Jesus intentionally addressed the man in John 5 who had been disabled for 38 years? Did Jesus's focus on this man, isolated from the community because of his disability, confuse the disciples?

2. The child represents people of any age who possess certain characteristics. What characteristics bring pleasure to God? How would you rate yourself on these characteristics?

3. Humbling oneself like a little child means relinquishing attitudes of self-importance or prideful ambition and recognizing our dependence on God. Are you more like the disciples, seeking positions of importance in the kingdom, or are you like the little child?

4. The kingdom belongs to those who receive it as a gift, without presumption of deserving God's grace and mercy. People with disabilities may appreciate this gift more than able-bodied persons. Could their disability then be a gift, or blessing, from God?

5. Jesus's teaching makes clear God's concern for those society overlooks. To be known as disciples of Jesus, what must be the Christian's response to people affected by disability?

6. To receive people in Jesus' name is to receive Jesus (18:5). What does "receiving" them mean in practical terms? How we treat the weakest, most impressionable, most oppressed and rejected, most vulnerable in society matters to God!

The Woman with a Hemorrhage: Luke 8:43–48

Luke tells us that this unnamed woman had been dealing with a problem of constant bleeding for 12 years without finding any help for her weakened condition. Her physical ailment (perhaps a menstrual or uterine problem) made her life difficult, but also affected her spiritually, since the flow of blood made her ceremonially unclean, disallowing her participation in the religious life of Israel (cf. Leviticus 15:19–25). Undoubtedly, she was discouraged and probably destitute, since she had seen many doctors who took her money but were unable to bring a cure (cf. Mark 5:26). Perhaps out of desperation, she approached Jesus as he passed through the crowd, seeking to touch the hem of his cloak and be healed. Tassels on Jewish men's garments were to remind them to obey God's commandments (Numbers 15:37–40; Deuteronomy 22:12). The Jews believed that the clothes of holy men could impart spiritual and curative power (Mark 6:56; Acts 19:11–12). Apparently she knew that Jesus had cured others and, out of desperation, now risked the crowds and public exposure to touch his garment, believing that this would result in a cure. Her faith was in being cured, though perhaps not in Jesus as Savior.

The woman did not allow the crowds or the thought that anyone she accidentally made contact with would become ceremonially unclean to keep her from touching the hem of Jesus's garment. Nor was she dissuaded by the fact that he was on his way to the house of Jairus. Like the four friends who brought the disabled men to Jesus by lowering him through the roof (Mark 2:1–12), no obstacle would prohibit her from reaching Jesus.

1. Was it culturally appropriate for her, because of her condition, to touch even the edge of Jesus's cloak? Were her actions based on fear that Jesus, being a Rabbi, would not touch her?

2. Her cure was immediate, perhaps making her instantly feel stronger. Any pain she might have had was gone. If you were this woman, how would you feel at that moment?

3. Jesus did not denounce her for her action, but he did ask that the person who touched him identify him- or herself. Surely Jesus knew who had been cured. Was his intent that she give testimony to her curing? Was it so that he could make it clear that there was nothing magical about his cloak? Was it to show that the ceremonial law that held her in bondage was ended through his ministry? What benefit was there to the woman in acknowledging that she had touched Jesus's cloak? What benefit was there to the crowds? Was it because Jesus knew that for her to be accepted by the community and welcomed into their worship, her cure would have to be made known (having had this ailment for 12 years, surely others would have known her condition and viewed her as "unclean").

4. This event is a reminder that suffering is not to be overlooked. This woman deserved attention and respect (even if a cure had not resulted). Jesus spoke to her gently and compassionately and told her to "go in peace" (more literally "go *into* peace"). Her cure was permanent. He gave her peace of both body and mind in restoring her to health. How would this blessing be "heard" by the woman? How was her life changed?

5. Is there anything in this woman's story that says her condition was linked to personal sin?

6. Are we like the crowds, "pressing in" on Jesus and preventing people with disabilities from reaching him?

The Rich Fool: Luke 12:13–21

In the parable, Jesus told of a farmer whose harvest was plentiful. The man said to himself that, having sufficient goods stored for many years, he should simply relax—eat, drink, and be merry. But God regarded the man as a fool, saying, "This night your soul is required of you, and the things you have prepared, whose will they be?" Jesus stated that rather than laying up treasure for ourselves, we should be "rich toward God." God made it clear that having an abundance of things is not what life is about.

Wiersbe (2001a) explained being rich toward God as gratefully acknowledging that all we have comes from God and is to be used for the good of others and the glory of God. Wiersbe understands being rich toward God to refer to *spiritual* enrichment, not just being rich with things that lead to personal enjoyment. It involves using whatever God provides to meet *his* priorities.

The farmer thought only about himself and his future. Jesus's story of the rich fool exposes the games people play to appear spiritual but who do not share God's priorities (Richards, 1987). God's priority is that we live a lifestyle of interacting with others that establishes a just relationship (cf. Micah 6:8 and Hosea 12:6). Jesus restated the Old Testament's emphasis on caring about others, specifically saying that this includes helping those who are poor and needy (Luke 12:33), and adding that "where your treasure is, there will your heart be also" (Luke 12:34).

1. Are you hoarding things which God has blessed you with instead of using them to bring glory to God and for compassionate ministry to others?

2. How does this teaching relate to people with disabilities and the Christian's need to reach out to families affected by disability?

3. Having gone through this entire study of ministering to and with persons affected by disability, list what you think are God's top five priorities for you and your church in ministry.

4. What does "being rich toward God" look like in disability ministry?

The Great Banquet: Luke 14:15–24

The teaching of Jesus in Luke 14:12–14 about not just partying with people who will reciprocate but instead inviting "the poor, the crippled, the lame, and the blind"—people who are not in a position to repay your kindness—is the lead-in to the parable of the great banquet. This passage is a mandate for disability ministry. The story is familiar to many: A wealthy man has planned a banquet to which the guests, despite having accepted the first invitation, now offer weak and unconvincing excuses for not coming. Their excuses would be quickly understood by Jesus's audience to be without merit. The host is angered and orders his servants to search through the city streets and the country lanes and byways to bring in those who were "outcasts" so that his banquet hall is filled.

This teaching clearly reveals the heart of God for people who have been marginalized by their society and neglected by the religious community. Consider the following as you think about how you and your church can become involved in disability ministry:

1. The people the servants now summoned to the banquet are invited to come *as they are*. There is no necessity for those with disabilities to be cured before they are welcomed to the feast. The parable helps us understand that compassionate care is more important than cure. How can you demonstrate this principle through ministry to people with disabilities?

2. The messengers are told to bring to the party the poor, the crippled, the lame, and the blind—representing all who are oppressed and cast aside by the rich and powerful. No excuses are acceptable. Many of these guests would need to be physically led to the banquet hall because of a visual impairment; others would need to be carried or otherwise transported to the master's house because of their physical disability. How can you or a team of volunteers from you church similarly assist persons with disabilities to gain access to God's "banquet hall?"

3. The master instructs his servants to *compel* the people to come. Social outcasts such as these would naturally assume that a mistake had been made, that the invitation was meant for someone else. They would have thought themselves unqualified to attend the banquet, or ashamed to come as a result of how they were viewed and treated by the able-bodied and wealthy of society. What is necessary to convince people affected by disability to understand that they are welcome at God's feast—that God loves them just as they are?

4. Where, in your community, can people with disabilities be found so that you can bring them to the banquet? What reasons might they have to distrust you when you reach out the them in Christ's love? How can you convince them of your sincerity in reaching out?

The Good Samaritan: Luke 10:25–27

This parable of Jesus is well known, but because of that its implications for disability ministry may be overlooked. The story is familiar: A man, presumably a Jew, is traveling from Jerusalem to Jericho. On his journey, he is attacked by thieves who beat him severely and leave him half-dead along the road. In time, a priest comes along the road, sees the man, and passes by on the far side of the road, perhaps to prevent becoming unclean should he touch the man and find that he is dead. Becoming unclean could be an embarrassment because of the necessity to follow the procedures required by the law to become cleansed. As time goes on, a Levite approaches but he, though not as bound by legal traditions, also passes by on the other side. Those listening to Jesus tell the story perhaps expected Jesus to next mention a good, respectable Jew to come along and assist the man. Instead, Jesus introduces a Samaritan traveler as the "hero" of the story. This man stopped, examined the man's condition, tended to his physical needs, transported him to the town (probably Jericho), and paid expenses for his lodging and care. Given the antagonism between Jews and Samaritans, this twist in the story was probably startling to those listening to Jesus.

The parable was occasioned by a question asked by an expert in Jewish law: "What shall I do to inherit eternal life?" Jesus asked him to answer his own question from the Law. The lawyer quoted Deuteronomy 6:5 and Leviticus 19:18, elsewhere referred to as the "Great Commandments." Though his answer was correct—love of God and neighbor is demanded by God—he could not admit that he had failed to live up to this requirement and sought to justify himself by asking Jesus to define *neighbor*.

Consider the following questions as you seek to understand what this passage has to say about ministry to people with disabilities. Let's change the scenario a bit and regard the injured man instead as a person with disabilities.

1. Who would those who passed by on the other side of the road represent? Note that the priest and the Levite are "church" folks. Would people from your church community respond to the disabled in the same way?

2. Who would the Samaritan represent? Consider his actions. Note the practical nature of what the Samaritan did to help the injured man. What corresponding actions could be offered to minister to someone who is disabled?

3. What is the difference between the attitude of the priest and Levite and that of the Samaritan?

4. What did it cost the man to take action to relieve the man's pain and suffering? Is there anything in Jesus's parable that suggests the Samaritan felt inconvenienced? How willing are you to expend your own funds to minister to the needs of someone with a disability? Caring for others, whether someone we know or a stranger in need, can be costly. But what does it cost _not_ to care, to intentionally miss the opportunity to be a good steward of what God has given us materially and spiritually?

5. Note how Jesus changed the question from "who is my neighbor?" to "who was neighbor to the man?" What is the significance of this change?

6. The parable shows what it means to show mercy as well as illustrating the ministry of Jesus. Summarize the implications of Jesus's teaching for ministry with persons who are disabled.

Judging Rightly: John 7:24

In this passage, Jesus said that we should not judge by appearances, but judge with right judgment—to "look beneath the surface so you can judge correctly" (NLT). Admittedly, this passage does not deal directly with issues of disability, but Jesus's statement is of significance to our study. Jesus's words echo God's counsel to Samuel when he sought to determine which of Jesse's sons he was to anoint as king of Israel. One of the issues discussed in this book is that people with disabilities are often thought to have little or no value, or to be sinners or people who are cursed. The presence of someone who has a "non-conventional body" often causes discomfort in temporally able-bodied persons because of lack of exposure to people who are disabled, or because of traditional lore and inaccurate information about disability coupled with not thinking biblically about disability. Judgment is made on the basis of appearance without taking time to get to know the person and family affected by disability. This judgment is often based on stereotyping and the supposition that people with the same disability are all alike. Jesus's words caution against judging by appearance—making unsupported assumptions about the person or persons.

1. Have you ever judged someone prematurely based on their appearance or on what you perceived their circumstances to be, but later found that you were grossly mistaken?

2. What does it mean to "judge with right judgment"? What does that require?

3. How do we break away from traditional, incorrect views of persons affected by disability?

4. What can you do to develop a relationship with individuals who are disabled in order to know them as *persons*? What is required for people to change from simply *seeing* the person to *looking at* the person with respect and the love of Christ"

5. What role can you play in helping others in your church and community to avoid making judgments on the basis of what seems to be rather than on knowledge gained through personal involvement with persons who are disabled?

Action Steps

Reflect on these passages from the perspective of disability ministry. What do they suggest in terms of what our attitudes should be toward and interaction with people affected by disability?

1. **John 13:34–35** "A new commandment I give to you, that you love one another: *just as I have loved you, you also are to love one another.* By this all people will know that you are my disciples, if you have love for one another." (Emphasis added)

   a. We are told to love as Jesus loved. How would you characterize the love of Jesus? How did he demonstrate his love for all people?

   b. What implications do you draw from this for doing ministry to and with persons who are disabled? What specific actions are required?

   c. What is the intended result of the action Jesus commanded in this passage? What should people (with or without disabilities) "see" as a result of our loving action toward others?

2. **Ephesians 5:1–2** "be imitators of God, as beloved children. And walk in love, as Christ loved us and gave himself up for us, a fragrant offering and sacrifice to God."

   a. This is a broad command from Paul that obviously applies to all of our life. It echoes the words of Jesus in John 13:34. What are its implications for approaching and interacting with individuals and families affected by disability?

   b. In what sense can ministry to and with persons with disabilities a "fragrant offering" to God? What specific actions can you make to contribute to that offering?

3. **1 Thessalonians 5:14** "And we urge you, brothers, admonish the idle, encourage the fainthearted, help the weak, be patient with them all."

   a. "Fainthearted" and "weak" may be characteristics of individuals and families affected by disability. To appropriately "encourage the fainthearted" and "help the weak" requires that you spend time with them in order to gain some insight into what they are experiencing and understand their needs and desires. But what general ideas come to mind that might be included in an encouraging and helpful approach to those affected by disability?

   b. How should a Christian "be" with (or "to") persons with disabilities? What are appropriate ways to respond to these individuals, even when they are unable to respond to you other than perhaps with a smile?

4. **Philippians 2:3–5** "Do nothing out of selfish ambition or vain conceit, but in humility consider others better than yourselves. Each of you should look not only to your own interests, but also to the interests of others. Your attitude should be the same as that of Christ Jesus." (NIV)

a. People who are able-bodied often feel superior to persons with disabilities. This becomes evident in how they look at, avoid, treat, or speak about the person, especially if the disability is multiple or severe. Have you found yourself looking down on someone who is disabled? What would it take for you to consider that person "better than yourself"?

b. "Selfish ambition or vain conceit" can be the basis for someone claiming that ministry to the disabled is a waste of time and resources because they will not be able to contribute in any way to the community of faith. How would you respond to someone—a member of the congregation or an uninformed church leader—who expresses such an opinion?

c. Being selfishly ambitious and conceited are the opposite of being compassionate and encouraging, and do not bring comfort, hope, and fellowship. But ambition and conceit seem to come more naturally to humankind. How can you break from that natural mode and, in a spirit of humility, minister to people with disabilities (and others)?

d. In what concrete ways can you "look to the interests" of individuals and families who are affected by disability? What is necessary to even become aware of "the interests" of these persons and families, to "forget yourselves long enough to lend a helping hand" (MSG)?

e. What attitude did Jesus display toward people who were marginalized because of disability or disease? How can you model that behavior today?

f. Able-bodied people may feel they are humbling themselves to serve people with disabilities. But they may, in fact, be humbled as they become aware of the inner strength, courage, and grace, and the deeper faith and dependence on God many people with disabilities display. How can you keep yourself open to learn *from* people with disabilities even as you seek to minister to them?

5. **Galatians 5:22–23** "But the fruit of the Spirit is love, joy, peace, patience, kindness, goodness, faithfulness, gentleness, self-control; against such things there is no law."

a. This is another passage in which Paul gives instruction regarding the behavior of Christians. The contrast with the "works of the flesh" (vv. 19–21) is also inescapably clear. But whereas *we* must lay aside the works of the flesh, it is the *Holy Spirit* who produces the fruit as we grow closer to the Lord (and, as we grow closer to the Lord, the fruit becomes "sweeter"). "Fruit" is singular; all those Paul mentions are part of the "bunch." Though the gifts of the Spirit vary among believers, each Christian is to be characterized by the fruit of the Spirit. Note, too, how each aspect of the fruit of the Spirit corresponds to the character of God and were displayed in the life of Jesus Christ.

b. As you consider each aspect of the Spiritual fruit, how do you see them applying to ministry to and with persons who are disabled?

    c. Which is more evident in your life—particularly in regard to people with disabilities: the fruit of the Spirit or the works of the flesh?

6. **Galatians 6:9–10** "And let us not grow weary of doing good, for in due season we will reap, if we do not give up. So then, as we have opportunity, let us do good to everyone, and especially to those who are of the household of faith."

    a. How can you put these words into action in working with people and families affected by disability?

Epilogue

I was going to call this section "final thoughts" but, since God continues to open my eyes to more Scripture passages that apply to or inform disability ministry, there can no final word, at least not until Jesus returns. I was reminded in church yesterday of Proverbs 29:18, which says "Where there is no revelation, people cast off restraint; but blessed is the one who heeds wisdom's instruction" (NIV). "Revelation" can be understood as *vision,* or *divine guidance.* Perhaps a more direct paraphrase is that given by Eugene Peterson: "If people can't see what God is doing, they stumble all over themselves; But when they attend to what he reveals, they are most blessed" (MSG).

One intended outcome of this book is that you gain a perspective on what God is doing or desires to do in and through disability and persons affected by disability. Biblically, this is seen in God's use of Paul and his disabling condition, his thorn. God loves to show his strength, power, love, and grace *in* and *through* human weakness. The crucifixion of Jesus Christ is a clear example of God's use of human frailty and what the world might consider foolishness to save a people and bring them into his kingdom.

It is my prayer that, having worked your way through this book, doing the reflection and "going deeper" activities, and spending time with the Scripture studies, your vision has been enlarged—your vision of what disability is, your vision of what God can do through people who are disabled, your vision of what God wants us to be (whether disabled or temporarily able-bodied), and your vision of hope in the Lord. When we attend to what God reveals, we will be blessed and we will be a blessing to others.

Ministry flows out of our desire to love and serve God. He has chosen us to be his hands and feet and voice in the world, proclaiming through word and deed his truth and his love to all peoples. People with disabilities are everywhere, though we often are "blind" to their presence. Let us be diligent in reaching out to them and bringing them into our fellowship in the family of God. Let us go with the same urgency as the master demanded in Jesus's parable in Luke 14 who sought to have his banquet hall filled: "Go out quickly to the streets and lanes of the city, and bring in the poor and crippled and blind and lame . . . . Go out to the highways and hedges and compel people to come in, that my house may be filled" (Luke 14:21–23).

My hope is that the church becomes a model for the world, a place where people of all races and cultures, people with abilities and disabilities, find a place to *be,* to worship in community, to use their gifts to glorify God and to serve one another is love.

References

Amegatcher, J. (2011). Psychosocial disability: Attitudes and barriers to social integration in church and society. In S. Kabue, E. Mombo & C. B. Peter (Eds.), *Disability, society, and theology: Voices from Africa* (pp. 275–295). Limuru, Kenya: Zapf Chancery Publishers Africa, LTD.

Anderson, G. (1985). Christian mission and human transformation: Toward century 21. *Mission Studies, 2*(1), 52–65.

Assemblies of God. (2000, August 11). *Position paper: Ministry to people with disabilities—A biblical perspective.* Retrieved from http://ag.org/top/Beliefs/Position_Papers/pp_downloads/pp_disabilities.pdf

Arora, K. (2009). Models of understanding chronic illness: Implications for pastoral theology and care. *Journal of Pastoral Theology, 17*(1), 22–37.

Barnes, A. (n.d.; originally published 1832). The Gospel of Matthew—Chapter 12. In R. Frew (Ed.), *Barnes's notes on the New Testament—Explanatory and Practical.* Colorado Springs, CO: WORDsearch CROSS e-book.

Beates, M. S. (2012). *Disability and the Gospel: How God uses our brokenness to display his grace.* Wheaton, IL: Crossway.

Benner, D. G. (1988). *Care of souls: Revisioning Christian nurture and counsel.* Grand Rapids, MI: Baker Books.

Black, K. (1996). *A Healing homiletic: Preaching and disability.* Nashville: Abingdon Press.

Boa, K. (2001). *Conformed to his image: Biblical and practical approaches to spiritual formation.* Grand Rapids, MI: Zondervan.

Browne, E. J. (1997). *The disabled disciple: Ministering in a church without barriers.* Ligouri, MO: Ligouri Publications.

Carder, M. M. (1984). Spiritual and religious needs of mentally retarded persons. *The journal of Pastoral Care, 38*(2), 143–154.

Chan, S. (1998). *Spiritual theology: A systematic study of the Christian life.* Downers Grove, IL: InterVarsity Press.

Clark, D. C., & Emmett, P. (1998). *When someone you live is dying: Making wise decisions at the end of life.* Minneapolis: Bethany Books.

Cooper, B. (1992). The disabled God. *Theology Today, 49*(2), 173–182.

Cope, M. (2011). *Megan's secrets: What my mentally disabled daughter taught me about life.* Abilene, TX: Leafwood Publishers.

Dahlstrom, R. (2011). *The color of hope: Becoming people of mercy, justice, and love*. Grand Rapids, MI: Baker Books.

Dawn, M. (2001). Suffering glory. *Journal for Preachers, 24*(3), 3–10.

DeYoung, C. P. (1997). *Reconciliation: Our greatest challenge, our only hope*. Valley Forge, PA: Judson Press.

Dignan, K., & Dignan, J. (2007). *Turning barriers into bridges*. Springfield MO: The General Council of the Assemblies of God. Retrieved from http://ag.org/top/church_workers/spcl_disabl_turning_barrie.cfm.

Dunavant, D. (2009, October). Man—Made in the image of God. *Journal of the Southern Baptist Convention, 10*, Retrieved from http://www.sbclife.org/articles/2009/2010/sla2006.asp.

Edmonds, M. (2011). *A theological diagnosis: A new direction on genetic therapy, 'disability' and the ethics of healing*. London, England: Jessica Kingsley Publishers.

Edwards, B. H. (Ed.) (2000). *Horizons of hope: Reality in disability*. Leominster, England: Day One Publications.

Eiesland, N. L. (1994). *The disabled God: Toward a liberatory theology of disability*. Nashville: Abingdon Press.

Eiesland, N. L. (2011, January-March). Liberation, inclusion and justice: A faith response to persons with disabilities. *Ecumenical Disability Advocates Network Quarterly Newsletter*, 18–21.

Estep, J. R. (2010). Christian anthropology: Humanity as the Image Dei. In J. R. Estep & J. H. Kim (Eds.), *Christian formation: Integrating theology and human development* (pp. 9–36). Nashville: B & H Academic.

Eugene, B. (1999). The church's evangelizing mission to the mentally handicapped. *AFER, 41*(1), 17–30.

Evans, T. (1998). *The battle is the Lord's*. Chicago: Moody Press.

Evans, T. (2002). *God is up to something good*. Sisters, OR: Multnomah Publishers.

Frazee, R. (2001). *The connecting church: Beyond small groups and authentic community*. Grand Rapids, MI: Zondervan.

Fritzen, A. (2011). Claiming and developing a disability hermeneutics: Toward a liberating theology of disability. In S. Kabue, E. Mombo, J. D. Galgalo & C. B. Peter (Eds.), *Disability, society, and theology: Voices from Africa* (pp. 25–29). Limuru, Kenya: Zapf Chancery Publishers Africa, LTD.

Fuller, W. H. (1987). The church and its mission and ministry. In P. Sookhedeo (Ed.), *New frontiers in missions*. (pp. 101–114). Grand Rapids, MI: Baker Books.

Gaventa, W. C., & Coulter, D. L. (Eds.). (2001). *The theological voice of Wolf Wolfensberger*. New York: Haworth Pastoral Press.

Habermas, R. T. (1993). Practical dimensions of the *Imago Dei*. *Christian Education Journal, 13*(2), 83–92.

Hardman, M., L., Drew, C. J., & Egan, M. W. (2011). *Human exceptionality: School, community, and family* (10th ed.). Belmont, CA: Wadsworth.

Harrison, T. (1995). *Disability: Rights and wrongs*. Oxford: Lion Publishing.

Hauerwas, S. (2004). Community and diversity: The tyranny of normality. In J. Swinton (Ed.), *Critical reflections of Stanley Hauerwas' theology of disability: Disabling society, enabling theology* (pp. 37–43). Binghamton, NY: Haworth Pastoral Press.

Hauerwas, S., & Willimon, W. H. (1989). *Resident aliens: A proactive Christian assessment of culture and ministry for people who know that something is wrong*. Nashville: Abingdon Press.

Hittenberger, J., & Mittelstadt, M. W. (2008). Review essay: Power and powerlessness in Pentecostal theology—A review essay on Amos Yong's "Theology and Down Syndrome: Reimaging disability in late modernity." *Pneuma, 30*(1), 137–145.

Hoekema, A. A. (1986). *Created in God's image*. Grand Rapids, MI: Eerdmans.

Hoeksema, T. (1990, December). One in the Spirit: Involving persons with disabilities in worship. *Reformed Worship: Resources for Planning and Leading Worship*. Retrieved from http://www.reformedworship.org/article/december-1990/one-spirit-involving-persons-disabilities-worship

Horne, S. (1998). "Those who are blind see": Some New Testament uses of impairment, inability, and paradox. In N. L. Eiesland & D. E. Saliers (Eds.), *Human disability and the service of God: Reassessing religious practice* (pp. 88–101). Nashville, TN: Abingdon Press.

Hubach, S. O. (2006). *Same lake, different boat*. Phillipsburg, NJ: P & R Publishing.

Keller, T. (2008). The Gospel in all its forms. *Leadership Journal*, Retrieved from *http://www.christianitytoday.com/le/2008/spring/9.74a.html*

Kirk, S., Gallagher, J. J., Coleman, M. R., & Anastasiow, N. J. (2012). *Educating exceptional children* (13th ed.). Belmont, CA: Wadsworth Publishing.

Kistemaker, S. J. (1980). *The parables: Understanding the stories Jesus told*. Grand Rapids, MI: Baker Books.

Kreeft, P. (1986). *Making sense out of suffering*. Ann Arbor, MI: Servant Books.

Lane, B. C. (1990). Grace and the grotesque. *Christian Century, 107*, 1067–1069.

Langer, R. (2011). Disability, calling and 'a kind of life imposed on man'. In J. E. Tada & S. Bundy (Eds.), *Beyond suffering: A Christian view on disability ministry*. Agoura Hills, CA: The Christian Institute on Disability, Joni and Friends International Disability Center.

Lewis, C. S. (1962). *The problem of pain*. New York: Macmillan.

Longchar, A. W. (2011). Sin, suffering, and disability in God's world. In S. Kabue, E. Mombo & J. D. Galgalo (Eds.), *Disability, Society, and Theology: Voices from Africa* (pp. 47–58). Limuru, Kenya: Zapf Chancery Publishers Africa, Ltd.

McCollum, A. B. (1998). Tradition, folklore, and disability: A heritage of inclusion. In N. L. Eiesland & D. E. Saliers (Eds.), *Human disability and the service of God: Reassessing religious practice* (pp. 167–186). Nashville: Abingdon.

Medina, K. (2006). *Finding God in autism.* Mustang, OK: Tate Publishing & Enterprises.

Meininger, H. P. (2001). Authenticity in community: Theory and practice of an inclusive anthropology in care for persons with intellectual disabilities. In W. C. Gaventa & D. L. Coulter (Eds.), *Spirituality and intellectual disability: International perspectives of the effect of culture and religion on healing body, mind, and soul* (pp. 13–28). New York: The Haworth Press.

Migliore, D. L. (2004). *Faith seeking understanding: An introduction to Christian theology* (2nd ed.). Grand Rapids, MI: Eerdmans.

Milne, B. (1993). *The message of John: Here is your king.* Downers Grove, IL: InterVarsity Press.

Mission Network News. (2011, 30 March). Church still has work to do with unreached people group. *http://www.mnnonline.org/article/15523.*

Moltmann, J. (1998). Liberate yourselves by accepting one another. In N. L. Eiesland & D. E. Saliers (Eds.), *Human disability and the service of God: Reassessing religious practice* (pp. 105–122). Nashville: Abingdon.

Mouw, R. (1992). *Uncommon decency: Christian civility in an uncivil world.* Downers Grove, IL: InterVarsity Press.

Murray, A. (1895). *Waiting on God* London: Nisbet & Co. WORDsearch CROSS e-book.

Naicker, S. (2003). Editorial. *EENET Newsletter, 7*, 1. Retrieved from http://www.eenet.org.uk/resources/eenet_newsletter/news7/page1.php.

Newell, C. (2010). On the importance of suffering: The paradox of disability. In H. S. Reinders (Ed.), *The paradox of disability: Responses to Jean Vanier and L'Arche Communities from theology and the sciences* (pp. 169–179). Grand Rapids, MI: Eerdmans.

Newman, G., & Tada, J. E. (1993). *All God's children: Ministry with disabled persons.* Grand Rapids, MI: Zondervan.

Nolan, A. (1976). *Jesus before Christianity.* Maryknoll, NY: Orbis Books.

Nouwen, H. J. M. (1975). *Reaching out: Three movements of the spiritual life.* New York: Image Books/Doubleday.

Nouwen, H. J. M. (1988). *The road to daybreak: A spiritual journey.* New York: Doubleday.

Nouwen, H. J. M. (1997). *Adam: God's beloved.* Maryknoll, NY: Orbis Books.

Onyinab, O. (2006). God's grace, healing and suffering. *International Review of Mission, 93*(376/377), 117–127.

Orr, J. (1939). *International Standard Bible Encyclopedia*. Retrieved from http://www.internationalstandardbible.com/J/justice.html

Osmer, R. R. (2008). *Practical theology: An introduction*. Grand Rapids, MI: Eerdmans.

Otieno, P. A. (2009). Biblical and theological perspectives of disability: Implications on the rights of persons with disability in Kenya. *Disability Studies Quarterly, 29*(4). Retrieved from http://dsq_sds.org/issue/view/42.

Packer, J. I., & Nystrom, C. (2000). *Never beyond hope: How God touches and uses imperfect people*. Downers Grove, IL: InterVarsity Press.

Palau, L. (1999). *Where is God when bad things happen?* New York: Doubleday.

Patterson, B. A. B. (1998). Redeemed bodies: Fullness of life. In N. L. Eiesland & D. E. Saliers (Eds.), *Human disability in the service of God: Reassessing religious practice* (pp. 123–143). Nashville: Abingdon.

Perkins, J. (1976). *A quiet revolution*. Waco, TX: Word.

Peter, C. B. (2011). One in Christ: Priesthood of the disabled and the exercising of gifts. In S. Kabue, E. Mombo & C. B. Peter (Eds.), *Disability, Society, and Theology: Voices from Africa* (pp. 59–77). Limuru, Kenya: Zapf Chancery Publishers Africa, LTD.

Petersen, J. (1993). *Lifestyle discipleship: The challenge of following Jesus in today's world*. Colorado Springs, CO: NavPress.

Pink, A. W. (1975). *Exposition of the gospel of John*. Grand Rapids, MI: Zondervan.

Piper, J. (1998). *God's passion for his glory*. Wheaton, IL: Crossways Books.

Piper, J. (2003). *Don't waste your life*. Wheaton, IL: Crossway Books.

Piper, J. (2012). *The pleasures of God: Meditations on God's delight in being God* (rev. ed.). Colorado Springs, CO: Multnomah Books.

Plantinga, C., Jr. (2002). *Engaging God's world: A vision of faith, learning, and living*. Grand Rapids, MI: Eerdmans.

Platt, D. (2010). *Radical: Taking back your faith from the American dream*. Colorado Springs, CO: Multnomah.

Pohl, C. D. (1995). Hospitality from the edge: The significance of marginality in the practice of welcome. *The Annual of the Society of Christian Ethics*, 121–136.

Pohl, C. D. (1999). *Making room: Recovering hospitality as a Christian tradition*. Grand Rapids, MI: Eerdmans.

Pohl, C. D. (2003). Biblical issues in mission and migration. *Missiology: An International Review, 31*(1), 1–15.

Pohl, C. D., & Buck, P. J. (2004). Hospitality and family life. *Family Ministry, 18*(3), 11–25.

Powlison, D. (2006). God's grace and your sufferings. In J. Piper & J. Taylor (Eds.), *Suffering and the sovereignty of God* (pp. 145–173). Wheaton, IL: Crossway Books.

Reinders, H. S. (2008). *Receiving the gift of friendship: Profound disability, theological anthropology, and ethics.* Grand Rapids, MI: Eerdmans.

Reinders, H. S. (2011). Is there meaning in disability? Or it is the wrong question? *Journal of Religion, Disability and Health, 15*(1), 57–71.

Reynolds, T. E. (2006). Welcoming without reserve? A case in Christian hospitality. *Theology Today, 6*(3), 191–202.

Reynolds, T. E. (2008). *Vulnerable communion: A theology of disability and hospitality.* Grand Rapids, MI: Brazos Press.

Richards, L. O. (1987). *The teacher's commentary.* Wheaton, IL: Victor Books. WORDsearch CROSS e-book.

Richards, L. O. (1999). *Encyclopedia of biblical words.* Grand Rapids, MI: Zondervan.

Roberts, J. D. (2002). Reconciliation with justice. *Perspectives in Religious Studies, 29*(4), 401–409.

Rowland, C., & Bennet, Z. (2006). "Action is the life of all": The Bible and practical theology. *Contact* (150), 8–17.

Russell, K. A. (2002, January-March). Out of weakness, strength; Out of sorrow comfort. *The Living Pulpit, 11*(1), 8–9.

Ryken, L., Wilhoit, J. C., & Longman, T., III (Eds.). (1998). *Dictionary of Biblical imagery.* Downers Grove, IL: InterVarsty Press.

Sanders, C. J. (1997). *Ministry at the margins: The prophetic mission of women, youth, and the poor.* Downers Grove, IL: InterVarsity Press.

Schramek, D. (2006). Waiting for the morning during the long night of weeping. In J. Piper & J. Taylor (Eds.), *Suffering and the sovereignty of God* (pp. 175–190). Wheaton, IL: Crossways Books.

Senior, D. (1995). Beware the Canaanite woman: Disabilities and the Bible. In M. E. Bishop (Ed.), *Religion and disability: Essays in scripture, theology, and ethics* (pp. 1–25). Kansas City, MO: Sheed and Ward.

Shelly, J. A. (2000). *Spiritual care: A guide for caregivers.* Downers Grove, IL: InterVarsity Press.

Shelly, J. A., & Miller, A. B. (1999). *Called to care: A Christian theology of nursing.* Downers Grove, IL: InterVarsity Press.

Sieck, T., & Hartvigsen, R. (2001). *How people with developmental disabilities can access the faith community of their choice.* Lakeside, CA: Home of the Guiding Hands.

Smart, J. (2001). *Disability, society, and the individual.* Austin, TX: Pro-Ed.

Sproul, R. C. (1988). *Surprised by suffering.* Wheaton, IL: Tyndale House.

Stearns, R. (2010). *The hole in the gospel.* Nashville: Thomas Nelson.

Stott, J. (1990). *Decisive issues facing Christians today.* Grand Rapids, MI: Fleming H. Revell.

Sullivan, P. M., & Knutson, J. F. (2000). Maltreatment and disabilities: A population-based epidemiological study. *Child Abuse & Neglect, 24*(10), 1257–1273.

Swinton, J. (1999). The politics of caring: Pastoral theology in an age of conflict and change. *Scottish Journal of Healthcare Chaplaincy, 2*(2), 25–30.

Swinton, J. (2000). *From bedlam to shalom: Towards a practical theology of human nature, interpersonal relationships and mental health care.* New York: Peter Lang.

Tada, J. E. (2010). *A place of healing: Wrestling with the mysteries of suffering, pain, and God's sovereignty.* Colorado Springs, CO: David C. Cook.

Tada, J. E., & Bundy, S. (2011). *Beyond suffering: A Christian view on disability ministry.* Agoura Hills, CA: The Christian Institute on Disability, Joni and Friends International Disability Center.

Tada, J. E., & Jensen, S. (1997). *Barrier-free friendships.* Grand Rapids, MI: Zondervan.

Tenny, M. C. (1953). *John: The gospel of belief.* Grand Rapids, MI: Eerdmans.

Tiffany, F. C., & Ringe, S. H. (1996). *Biblical interpretation: A roadmap.* Nashville, TN: Abingdon Press.

Truex, E. (1992). Compassion: Infiltrating the profession of nursing. *Direction Journal, 21*(1), 52–63. Retrieved from http://www.directionjournal.org/article?748

Vanier, J. (1992). *From brokenness to community.* Mahwah, NJ: Paulist Press.

Volf, M. (1996). *Exclusion and embrace: A theological exploration of identity, otherness, and reconciliation.* Nashville: Abingdon.

Vujicic, N. (2010). *Life without limbs: Inspiration for a ridiculously good life.* New York: Doubleday.

Walker, J. (2010). *Costly grace.* Abilene, TX: Leafwood Publishers.

Warrington, K. (2006, January/April). Healing and suffering in the Bible. *International Review of Mission, 95*(376/377), 154–164.

Watkins, D. R. (1994). *Christian social ministry: An introduction.* Nashville, TN: Broadman & Holman Publishers.

Webb-Mitchell, B. (1988). The place and power of acceptance in pastoral care with persons who are mentally retarded. *The Journal of Pastoral Care, 24*(4), 351–360.

Webb-Mitchell, B. (1994a). Make way for the electric blue wheelchair! Matthew 20:1–16. *Journal for Preachers, 17*(4), 36–28.

Webb-Mitchell, B. (1994b). *Unexpected guests at God's banquet: Welcoming people with disabilities into the church.* New York: The Crossroad Publishing Co.

Webb-Mitchell, B. (1996). *Dancing with disabilities: Opening the church to all God's children.* Cleveland, OH: United Church Press.

Wiersbe, W. W. (2001a). *The Bible exposition commentary—New Testament, Volume 1.* Colorado Springs, CO: Victor Books. WORDsearch CROSS e-book.

Wiersbe, W. W. (2001b). *The Bible exposition commentary—New Testament, Volume 2.* Colorado Springs, CO: Victor Books. WORDsearch CROSS e-book.

Wiersbe, W. W. (2001c). *The Bible Exposition Commentary—Pentateuch.* Colorado Springs, CO: Victor Books. WORDsearch CROSS e-book.

Wiersbe, W. W. (2004). *The Bible exposition commentary—Wisdom and Poetry.* Colorado Springs, CO: Victor Books. WORDsearch CROSS e-book.

Wink, W. (1995). "Normalcy" as disease: Facing disabilities. *Church and Society, 85*(5), 10–17.

Wolfensberger, W. (1972). *Normalization: The Principle of Normalization in human services.* Toronto: National Institute on Mental Retardation.

Wolfensberger, W. (1983). Social Role Valorization: a proposed new term for the principle of normalization. *Mental Retardation, 21*(6), 234–239.

Wolfensberger, W. (2000). A brief overview of Social Role Valorization. *Mental Retardation, 38*(2), 105–123.

World Health Organization. (2011). *World disability report.* Geneva, Switzerland: World Health Organization.

World Health Organization. (2011). *World disability report.* Geneva, Switzerland: World Health Organization.

Wright, N. T. (2006). *Evil and the justice of God.* Downers Grove, IL: InterVarsity Press.

Yancey, P. (1990). *Where is God when it hurts?* Grand Rapids, MI: Zondervan.

Yong, A. (2007). *Theology and down syndrome: Reimagining disability in late modernity.* Waco, TX: Baylor University Press.

Yong, A. (2011). *The Bible, disability, and the church: A new vision of the people of God.* Grand Rapids, MI: Eerdmans.

Zacharias, R. (1988). *Cries of the heart: Bringing God near when he feels so far.* Nashville: Word Publishing.

Zorrilla, H. (1988). *The good news of justice. Share the gospel: Live justly.* Scottsdale, PA: Herald Press.

Suggested readings for further study of disability and related issues:

Block, J. W. (2000). *Copious hosting: A theology of access for people with disabilities.* New York: Continuum.

Carter, E. W. (2007). *Including people with disabilities in faith communities.* Baltimore: Paul H. Brookes Publishing Co.

Eiesland, N. L., & Saliers, D. E. (1998). *Human disability and the service of God: Reassessing religious practice.* Nashville, TN: Abingdon Press.

Osborn, S. T., & Mitchell, J. L. (2004). *A special kind of love: For those who love children with special needs.* Nashville: Broadman & Holman Publishers.

Pierson, J. O. (1998). *No disabled souls: How to welcome people with disabilities into your life and your church.* Cincinnati, OH: Standard.

Books the Present New Exemplars for Understanding People with Disabilities

Bonker, E. M., & Breen, V. G. (2011). *I am in here: The journey of a child with autism who cannot speak but finds her voice.* Grand Rapids, MI: Revell.

Brown, C. (1996, 2003). *I am what I am by the grace of God.* Warsaw, OH: Echoing Hills Village Foundation.

Cope, M. (2011). *Megan's secrets: What my mentally disabled daughter taught me about life.* Abilene, TX: Leafwood Publishers.

DeVinck, C. (1988). *The power of the powerless: A brother's legacy of love.* New York: The Crossroads Publishing Co.

Tada, J. E. (2009). *A lifetime of wisdom: Embracing the God heals you.*

Vujicic, N. (2010). *Life without limbs: Inspiration for a ridiculously good life.* New York: Doubleday.